BANK MERGERS, ACQUISITIONS

STRATEGIC ALLIANCES

POSITIONING & PROTECTING YOUR BANK IN THE ERA OF CONSOLIDATION

HAZEL J. JOHNSON

A Bankline Publication

Professional Publishing*
Burr Ridge, Illinois
New York, New York

A BankLine Publication

ISBN 1-55738-746-X

Printed in the United States of America

BB

1 2 3 4 5 6 7 8 9 0

HCC

In Loving Memory of
Ida W. Kelly and Lucille V. Johnson

Bank Mergers, Acquisitions and Strategic Alliances: At a Glance

Chapters

Appendixes

Contents

6. Valuation Techniques, Part II: Off-Balance Sheet Categories and Fee Income 181

Preface

The banking industry is consolidating at an unprece-
dented pace. In the 1980s, bank failures precipitated
much of the consolidation. But in the 1990s, shrinkage in
the industry is more often associated with competitive
factors and the changing regulatory environment. In fact,
competition in the banking industry has never been more
intense. Blue-chip corporate clients can easily obtain
financing through the securities market. Middle-market
businesses can turn to finance companies, such as
General Electric Capital Corporation (GECC), that are
subject to far fewer regulations. Retail customers may
now choose from a wide range of nonbank financial institutions that can deliver services efficiently without brick-
and-mortar branches. To meet these competitive challenges, "cost containment" and "efficiency" have become
the watch words of the banking industry. One of the best
ways to achieve these goals is to increase client base,
without significantly increasing overhead. Mergers and
acquisitions have become an industry-wide response to
competitive threats. Also fueling this feeding frenzy is

the 1994 passage of the Riegle-Neal Interstate Banking and Branching Efficiency Act, which permits nationwide branching no later than 1997. In 1975, there were over 14,000 U.S. commercial banks. By 1994, the number had declined to 10,592. It has been estimated that consolidation in the industry will reduce that number to 5,000.

Essentially, every bank must consider itself either an acquirer or an acquisition target. The form of combination can be a merger or an acquisition. In a merger, the managements of the two institutions usually consent and work out a collaborative arrangement with respect to combined bank. For each institution contemplating a merger, the relevant questions are:

- When is the right time to merge?
- How do you identify the right partner?
- How do you successfully communicate the benefits of the merger to market analysts?
- How do you approach consolidating the two banks?

A merger is called an *acquisition* when one of the banks in the transaction, usually the larger, takes over the other institution and consolidates the two organizations into a single entity. The acquirer's name is usually retained and control of the decision making process rests almost entirely with the acquirer. A successful acquisition strategy will include additional guidelines for:

- Assembling the right acquisition team
- Narrowing the field of acquisition targets
- Designing strategies to approach the acquisition target
- Deciding on the use of brokers and finders

At the same time, it is not always necessary or desirable to take an equity position in another firm to expand market share in the current geographic area of operation, to enter new geographic areas, to offer new products, or to operate more efficiently. If the advantage of working with another firm appears to be an advantage that may diminish with time, a *strategic alliance* is more appropriate. Such arrangements can be particularly useful when a bank seeks efficiency improvements and new product offerings.

To properly execute a merger or acquisition, the price of the institution should be based on an objective assessment of value. Valuation techniques center around the institution's balance sheet—the assets and liabilities that represent future cash flows. Increasingly, the rights and obligations that are not recorded on the balance sheet have assumed a more significant role—credit commitments, swaps, forward contracts, and other option-like instruments that often are collectively referred to as derivatives. At one time, noninterest income was composed primarily of service charges on deposits and trust fees. Now noninterest income is much more varied, including fees from brokerage activities, mutual fund sales, servicing assets after sales, and corporate finance. Arguably, off-balance sheet and fee-generating activities represent the greatest potential for growth in the banking industry and are vital parts of the valuation process.

Bank Mergers, Acquisitions, and Strategic Alliances provides a framework for analyzing all of these issues—from both quantitative and qualitative perspectives. The guidelines in the book facilitate the fundamental decision to merge or acquire, identification of the right partner, proper valuation of the institution, consolidation of the two institutions, and the critical communications process. In the case of strategic alliances, *Bank Mergers, Acquisitions, and Strategic Alliances* provides insights into increasing efficiency and offering new products through less formal ties with other banks and with nonfinancial corporations. Also included are case studies that examine mergers and acquisitions by a number of institutions: NationsBank, Chemical Banking, BankAmerica, Banc One, PNC, and Fleet Financial. Other illustrations of bank strategies highlight Signet Bank, KeyCorp, First Tennessee Bank, National Australia Bank, Multinet International Bank, Countrywide Home Mortgage Loan Corporation, Liberty Bancorp of Oklahoma, and Zion Bancorp in Utah. Thus, *Bank Mergers, Acquisitions and Strategic Alliances* provides both the framework and the illustrations that support the decision making process in this critical area.

The companion software facilitates implementation of the concepts described in *Bank Mergers, Acquisitions and Strategic Alliances*, including analysis of valuation, profitability of the merged institution, potential cost savings, and comparative strengths. A description of the software is provided in Appendix C. This software is available through Global Bank Research (502-423-0760).

Clearly, continued consolidation in the banking industry is inevitable. Bank managers should take advantage of the tremendous opportunities for growth in this new environment of U.S. commercial banking.

Hazel J. Johnson, Ph.D., C.P.A.

1

The Bank Consolidation Phenomenon

Introduction

NationsBank Chairman Hugh McColl called it "a victory for bank customers everywhere."[1] He was referring to the passage of the Interstate Banking Bill by the U.S. Senate. The bill ushers in nationwide banking for the entire country for the first time since passage of the 1927 McFadden Act. Bank customers will be able to conduct banking business at any location of their bank, without regard to state boundaries. A direct effect of this new federal legislation will be to sustain the already strong momentum of the consolidation trend in the U.S. banking industry.

Structural Changes in the Industry

As recently as 1975, U.S. banks numbered over 14,000. The number of banks was relatively stable even in light of the difficult economic conditions produced by the hyper-

Exhibit 1–1
Number of U.S. Banks

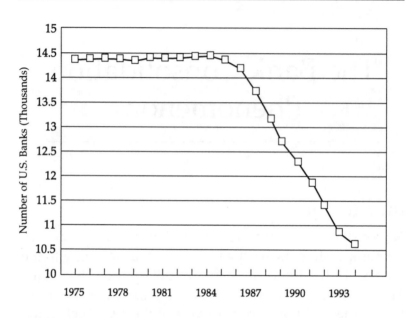

Source: Global Bank Research, based on data from: *FDIC Statistics on Banking,* various years.

inflation of the early 1980s. However, as illustrated in Exhibit 1–1, the number began to decline precipitously in the mid-1980s. By 1994, the number of U.S. banks was down to 10,592. Early consolidation in the industry resulted primarily from bank failures that rose from less than 20 per year in the 1940-to-1980 period to over 200 per year by the late 1980s. Since that time, the failure rate has declined significantly to 72 in 1992 and only 42 in 1993. In fact, the banking industry posted record profits in 1993.

Nevertheless, the industry continues to shrink. Exhibit 1–2 shows that the level of merger activity has increased from less than 100 in 1975 to a high of 800 in 1988 to a current average of approximately 500 per year. It has been projected that this merger and acquisition trend will end only when the number of U.S. banks is closer to 5,000.

Exhibit 1–2

U.S. Bank Mergers

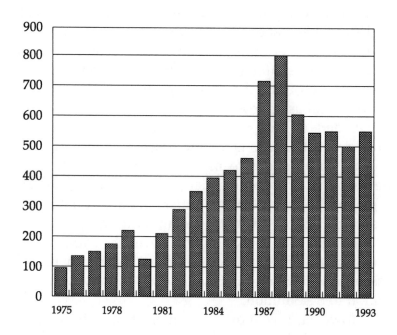

Source: Global Bank Research, based on data from: *FDIC Statistics on Banking,* various years.

Reasons for the Consolidation Trend

Since banks are no longer failing at the rate that they
have in the past, a natural question is "Why should the
banking industry continue to contract?" The answer lies
in the competitive environment of commercial banks.
Historically, banks have played a central role in the payments system and been the primary source of short-term
finance for industry. In 1964, banks and other depository institutions held 58% of the total assets of financial
institutions.[2] Twenty-five years later, their share had
dropped to 49%. The growth of pension funds and
investment companies (both mutual funds and closed
end funds) is responsible for this decline in bank asset
holdings. Furthermore, since investment companies and
securities firms offer accounts functionally equivalent to
checking accounts, the shrinkage has also occurred in
the deposit base of commercial banks.

Added to this increased competition from other
financial institutions is the increased tendency of nonfinancial corporations to meet their short-term financial
needs by issuing commercial paper, effectively bypass-
ing bank loans. In 1983, commercial paper outstanding
was $184 billion. By 1993, the amount had grown at a
12% annual rate to $554 billion. Over the same period,
the growth of commercial and industrial loans was
essentially stagnant, increasing only slightly from $404
billion to $443 billion.

However, low short-term interest rates in the early
1990s provided banks with comfortable margins. In fact,
1993 was a record year for the industry, with net income
of $43 billion, as compared to $32 billion in 1992, $18 bil-

lion in 1991, and $16 billion in 1990. But when interest rates began to rise in early 1994, bank spreads narrowed. The higher rates on mortgage and consumer loans put a damper on loan demand, with mortgage lending declining by 25% in 1994.

At the same time, the buildup of bank capital is exerting pressure on returns on equity. In 1988, banking industry capital was 6.3% of assets. By 1993, capital strength had increased to 8% of year-end assets, a level that the industry continues to maintain currently. This strong capital base will tend to push the larger banks into one of two directions. Higher dividends and stock buy backs can boost returns on equity—but only to a small degree. It is much more likely that the big institutions will leverage their balance sheets and accelerate the pace of their mergers and acquisitions. In the case of smaller banks, which are less likely to engage in balance-sheet leveraging and aggressive acquisitions, the reaction will likely be much more straightforward—many will sell the bank to the highest bidder. Thus, the industry's healthy capital base undoubtedly will help fuel the feeding frenzy.

All these market forces have caused banks to look for ways to become more efficient in their operations to boost the bottom line and returns on equity. "Cost control" is a paramount concern in this push for greater efficiency. By early 1995, many banks, including Chemical Banking, Chase Manhattan, and Fleet Financial had announced major cuts in employment rolls. Employment in the banking industry has declined from 2.2 million in 1989 to less than 2 million currently.

Clearly, one of the best ways to become more efficient is expand customer base without a comparable

expansion in administrative expense. It has been estimated that a merger of two banks in different markets
can produce cost savings of 10% to 15%. A merger
between two institutions with redundant branches can
yield savings of 35% or more. Thus, the synergies available through mergers and acquisitions can help commercial banks deliver more cost-effective services.

The Diversification Incentive

In meeting competition from nonbank financial service
providers, acquiring firms for diversification also has
considerable appeal. Through special regulatory permission from the Federal Reserve, commercial banks may
operate securities subsidiaries, as long as underwriting
revenue is limited to 10% or less of the subsidiary's
income. The business of corporate securities issuance
has not suffered the same stagnation as corporate lending. In 1983, corporate bonds outstanding amounted to
$643 billion. By 1993, this total had increased at a 13%
annual rate to $2.27 trillion.

Banks have taken the approach of moving into more diversified operations. Banks such as PNC
Bank Corporation and BankAmerica have recently
acquired mortgage banking businesses. Other banks
are acquiring leasing companies or opening offices in
supermarkets to sell mutual funds and annuities. Some
bankers are quite vehement about this diversification
push. Richard Kovacevich, CEO of Norwest Corporation, leaves little doubt about his sentiments when he
says, "I would emphatically say that the banking
industry is dead."[3]

Hugh L. McColl, Jr. of NationsBank has elaborated on this theme of change in the banking industry, including the resulting consolidation:

> In short, the banking business is in secular decline . . . From Merrill Lynch to IBM to GE, everyone has their finger in the financial services pie. Today, you can get VISA credit cards from British Petroleum or Fidelity and earn points on them toward gas or mutual funds. Or, you can get a home equity loan from Ford. Even computer whiz Bill Gates wants in on the action. He talks about "by-passing" banks through personal computers and—quote—"transforming the world financial system." "A pot of gold," he calls it.
>
> *All* of these non-bank competitors today have customers that once belonged to banks. *None* of them is hampered by the burdensome regulations that come with a bank charter . . . But, for now, that's our problem, not the customer's. And what the customer has made clear is that he will not pay for costly overhead. He is not in the mood to pay for the costs of banking regulation. And he will not pay for the banking industry's overcapacity.
>
> So we have one sure response. To bring the industry's costs in line with what the customer WILL pay for. That means the industry will continue to consolidate to gain efficiency. The question is not if. Or when. But how fast.[4]

State Laws and Regional Pacts

The process of consolidation has also been facilitated by individual state laws. Gradually, in-state branching and interstate banking laws at the state level have been liberalized.

Exhibit 1–3
State Branching Laws

Unit (1)

Colorado

Limited (8)

Illinois	Minnesota
Iowa	Missouri
Kentucky	New Mexico
Louisiana	Tennessee

Statewide (42)

Alabama[1]	Idaho	Nevada	Rhode Island
Alaska	Indiana[1]	New Hampshire	South Carolina
Arizona	Kansas[1]	New Jersey	South Dakota
Arkansas[2]	Maine	New York	Texas
California	Maryland	North Carolina	Utah
Connecticut	Massachusetts	North Dakota[1]	Vermont
Delaware	Michigan	Ohio	Virginia
District of Columbia	Mississippi	Oklahoma[1]	Washington
Florida[1]	Montana[1]	Oregon	West Virginia
Georgia[1]	Nebraska[1]	Pennsylvania	Wisconsin
Hawaii			Wyoming[1]

1   Statewide branching by merger.
2   After December 31, 1998.

Source: U.S. Department of the Treasury. *Modernizing the Financial System; Recommendations for Safer, More Competitive Banks*, 1991, p. XVII–7.

Branching Laws

The federal McFadden Act of 1927 gives national banks the right to branch within the state to the same extent that state banks are permitted to branch. There are generally three categories of branching powers:

- *Unit-banking* states permit no branching whatsoever.
- *Statewide branching* states permit branching throughout the state.
- *Limited branching* states permit some branching, but not statewide branching.

Exhibit 1–3 classifies each state and the District of Columbia according to these guidelines. The only remaining unit banking state is Wyoming. Eight states permit limited branching while the remaining states permit statewide branching. In some cases, statewide branching is permissible only through mergers.

A 1985 branch approval decision by the Comptroller of the Currency has had the effect of further liberalizing the branching laws of individual states. In a case involving Mississippi, the Comptroller ruled that the state had given thrift institutions the same powers as state banks and, thus, the state thrifts could be regarded as state banks for purposes of interpreting the McFadden Act. This decision permitted a *national bank* to branch according to the more liberal standards that had been established for state-chartered thrifts. In turn, the decision led a number of state banking regulators to grant *state banks* the same branching privileges as state thrifts.

Interstate Banking

Until the new federal interstate banking law is effective, state law will continue to dictate the extent to which bank holding companies can expand across state lines. The bank holding company structure has been instrumental in effecting interstate banking since the mid-1950s when interstate banking was discouraged by federal legislation.

The Bank Holding Company Act stipulates that states may impose limits on holding company acquisitions of banks within state boundaries. All states permit multibank holding companies. Limitations of bank holding companies acquisitions take various forms, including specific geographic restrictions, a maximum share of state deposits, or a maximum number of acquisitions for a specified period of time. However, some states place no limits on holding company acquisitions of banks. Since, until now, state and federal laws have prohibited branching across state lines, interstate acquisitions of banks have been accomplished largely through holding company acquisitions.

The Douglas Amendment of the Bank Holding Company Act of 1956 prohibits interstate acquisition of banks by bank holding companies unless specifically authorized by the laws of the state in which the acquired bank is located. In 1956, no state had any such laws and cross-border acquisitions were effectively halted.[5]

In 1975, Maine became the first state to permit acquisition of a bank by an out-of-state holding company. However, the Maine law required reciprocity. That is, no out-of-state holding company could buy a bank in Maine unless a Maine holding company could also buy a bank in the home state of the acquiring institution.

Exhibit 1–4
State Laws Concerning Interstate Banking

No Law (1)
Hawaii

Nationwide Entry (12)

Alaska	Idaho	New Hampshire	Texas
Arizona	Maine	New Mexico	Utah
Colorado	Nevada	Oregon	Wyoming

Nationwide Entry, with Reciprocity (22)

California	Louisiana	New York	Rhode Island
Connecticut	Massachusetts	North Dakota	South Dakota
Delaware	Michigan	Ohio	Tennessee
Illinois	Nebraska	Oklahoma[1]	Vermont
Indiana	New Jersey	Pennsylvania	Washington
Kentucky			West Virginia

Regional Reciprocal Entry Only (16)

State	Region	Reciprocal States
Alabama	13 states and DC	Arkansas, Florida, Georgia, Kentucky, Louisiana, Maryland, Mississippi, North Carolina, South Carolina, Tennessee, Texas, Virginia, West Virginia, DC

Exhibit 1–4
State Laws Concerning Interstate Banking (cont.)

Arkansas	16 states and DC	Alabama, Florida, Georgia, Kansas, Louisiana, Maryland, Missouri, Mississippi, North Carolina, Nebraska, Oklahoma, South Carolina, Tennessee, Texas, Virginia, West Virginia, DC
District of Columbia	11 states	Alabama, Florida, Georgia, Louisiana, Maryland, Mississippi, North Carolina, South Carolina, Tennessee, Virginia, West Virginia
Florida	11 states and DC	Alabama, Arkansas, Georgia, Louisiana, Maryland, Mississippi, North Carolina, South Carolina, Tennessee, Virginia, West Virginia, DC
Georgia	10 states and DC	Alabama, Florida, Kentucky, Louisiana, Maryland, Mississippi, North Carolina, South Carolina, Tennessee, Virginia, DC
Iowa	6 states	Illinois, Minnesota, Missouri, Nebraska, South Dakota, Wisconsin
Kansas	6 states	Arkansas, Colorado, Iowa, Missouri, Nebraska, Oklahoma

Exhibit 1–4
State Laws Concerning Interstate Banking (cont.)

Maryland	14 states and DC	Alabama, Arkansas, Delaware, Florida, Georgia, Kentucky, Louisiana, Mississippi, North Carolina, Pennsylvania, South Carolina, Tennessee, Virginia, West Virginia, DC
Minnesota	16 states	Colorado, Iowa, Idaho, Illinois, Indiana, Kansas, Michigan, Missouri, Montana, North Dakota, Nebraska, Ohio, South Dakota, Washington, Wisconsin, Wyoming
Mississippi	13 states	Alabama, Arkansas, Florida, Georgia, Kentucky, Louisiana, Missouri, North Carolina, South Carolina, Tennessee, Texas, Virginia, West Virginia
Missouri	8 states	Arkansas, Iowa, Illinois, Kansas, Kentucky, Nebraska, Oklahoma, Tennessee
Montana	7 states	Colorado, Idaho, Minnesota, North Dakota, South Dakota, Wisconsin, Wyoming
North Carolina	13 states and DC[2]	Alabama, Arkansas, Florida, Georgia, Kentucky, Louisiana, Maryland, Mississippi, South Carolina, Tennessee, Texas, Virginia, West Virginia, DC

Exhibit 1–4
State Laws Concerning Interstate Banking (cont.)

South Carolina	12 states and DC	Alabama, Arkansas, Florida, Georgia, Kentucky, Louisiana, Maryland, Mississippi, North Carolina, Tennessee, Virginia, West Virginia, DC
Virginia	12 states and DC	Alabama, Arkansas, Florida, Georgia, Kentucky, Louisiana, Maryland, Mississippi, North Carolina, South Carolina, Tennessee, West Virginia, DC
Wisconsin	8 states	Iowa, Illinois, Indiana, Kentucky, Michigan, Minnesota, Missouri, Ohio

1   After initial entry, BHC must be from state offering reciprocity or wait 4 years to expand.
2   After July 1, 1996, becomes national entry, with reciprocity.

Source: LaWare, John P. Member, Board of Governors of the Federal Reserve System, Statement Before the Committee on Banking, Housing and Urban Affairs, United States Senate, October 5, 1993.

Since there were no other states with such statutes, no out-of-state acquisitions of Maine banks resulted.

However, beginning in the early 1980s, additional states began to enact laws that permitted acquisitions by out-of-state holding companies. The laws in Alaska, Massachusetts, and New York became effective in 1982. Since that time, all states except Hawaii have enacted some form of interstate bank holding company legislation.

Interstate banking, with the attendant mergers and acquisitions, received considerable momentum by individual state laws and regional pacts. Thirty-four states now provide for the acquisition of their banks by out-of-state holding companies from any other state.

Exhibit 1–4 summarizes the status of interstate banking laws for all states and the District of Columbia. The four general classifications are:

- *No law.* The state does not have a law that permits the purchase of banks by out-of-state bank holding companies (BHCs).
- *Nationwide entry.* The state allows BHCs from any other state to acquire its banks.
- *Nationwide entry, with reciprocity.* In some cases, reciprocity (the right for BHCs in the state of the acquired bank to do the same in the state of the acquiring BHC) is required.
- *Regional reciprocal entry only.* Within a selected group of states, each state permits the acquisition of its banks by BHCs headquartered in the other states of the group as long as each state has the same right.

Hawaii is the only state without an interstate banking law. There are 12 states that permit nationwide entry by BHCs and 22 that permit nationwide entry with reciprocity. Another 16 states permit entry only by BHCs domiciled in states with which there is a reciprocal agreement.

New England and the Southeast have been particularly active in forming regional pacts. The intent of these arrangements is to permit local institutions to consolidate and strengthen their operations in preparation for truly nationwide banking. As a result, New York money-center banks have been excluded from regional pacts.

Until the federal interstate banking law is effective, state branching and interstate banking laws will continue to govern mergers and acquisitions of existing banking facilities.

Federal Regulation of Mergers and Acquisitions

The Bank Merger Act was passed to clarify the antitrust policies that apply to bank mergers. The act amended the Federal Deposit Insurance Corporation Act to stipulate that a bank could not merge, acquire assets or liabilities of, or consolidate with another bank without prior approval of the appropriate supervisory bodies.[6]

Exhibit 1–5

Regulatory Approval of Mergers and Acquisitions: Factors Considered by Supervisory Bodies

---

- Financial condition and history of each bank involved in the merger
- Capital adequacy
- Future earnings prospects
- Bank management
- Convenience and needs of the community to be served
- Effects on competition

Source: Spong, Kenneth. *Banking Regulation: Its Purposes, Implementation, and Effects.*

The factors to be considered by each of the supervisory bodies are included in Exhibit 1–5. Regulators consider the financial factors, capital adequacy, future earnings, bank management, the community being served, and competitive effects.

In terms of the financial condition of each bank, regulators review the balance sheet and income statement of the acquiring bank, the acquired bank, and the resultant bank, that is, the bank that will emerge after the combination is complete. If one of the bank's has had a poor earnings record, the resultant bank is scrutinized more closely. If the acquiring bank is assuming deposits with little or no assumption of assets, the degree of leverage of the resultant bank is reviewed to determine that capital will be adequate. Particular attention is given to the adequacy of loan loss reserves. Pro forma income statements are prepared and reviewed. However, it is understood that these are merely projections and more emphasis is placed on the balance sheet of the resultant bank. Nevertheless, if future earnings can be determined to be weak, suspect, or doubtful, the application may not be approved.

Bank management is considered in terms of the ability to manage the resultant institution. This review is made somewhat easier when the management of the acquiring institution is known to the regulators performing the review. An application probably will not be approved if the resultant institution will continue with weak or unsatisfactory management. Also, particular attention is paid to the existence of any insider transactions and any inducement to any officer, director, or employee to promote or encourage the merger.

The needs and convenience of the community being served are considered in terms of the availability of banking services in the relevant geographic market. Generally, the test is whether expected benefits can be achieved through other, less anticompetitive means. In the case of a combination of two banks in different geographic markets, this test is generally not difficult to pass. Even if the combination involves two institutions in the same market, the elimination of redundant branches can generally be justified if the branches are in very close proximity. Benefits that will often accrue to the community include higher lending limits of the resultant bank, new and expanded services, and reduced prices. Another important test with respect to the community being served is the acquiring institution's compliance with the Community Reinvestment Act (CRA). If the rating has not been "satisfactory," regulators require appropriate commitments or efforts at improvement of the rating.[7]

Competitive factors are determined by reference to:

- Geographic market
- Product market
- The extent of the lessening of competition

The relevant geographic market consists of those areas in which the merging institutions are located and from which they derive the predominant portion of their loan, deposit, or other business. The relevant market also includes the areas where their customers (existing and potential) may bind alternative banking services. If possible, the relevant geographic market is defined in terms of political subdivisions (cities, counties, states) to facilitate statistical analysis.

Product market considerations include the products offered by the resultant institution and by the competitors of the resultant institution. The competitors can include nonbank institutions. For example, thrifts offer the equivalent of demand deposit checking accounts in the form of negotiable order of withdrawal (NOW) accounts. Captive finance companies of automobile manufacturers offer automobile loans, mortgage banks offer residential mortgage loans, and business finance companies offer corporate loans. The availability of banking services will be analyzed in this context.

With respect to the issue of lessened competition, the Bank Merger Act was amended in 1966 to provide the standard that all banking agencies and the Justice Department must use in assessing the impact of mergers. No merger can be approved that would result in a monopoly or that would substantially lessen competition. The review includes an assessment of the degree of concentration among competing firms in the relevant geographic market. The measure that is used to assess the extent of lessening of competition is the Herfindahl-Hirschman Index (HHI). In applying the HHI, the market share (in percentage terms) of each competing firm is determined and then squared. The sum of these squared market shares is the HHI. In a market in which there is only one competitor, the HHI will be 10,000 (100^2). A high HHI implies a highly concentrated market and makes it more likely that the Justice Department will challenge a proposed merger of banks. A low HHI implies a less concentrated market and the Justice Department is not as likely to challenge a bank merger. Specifically, if a combination of banks creates an HHI that is greater than 1800 or an

HHI that increases by more than 200, the competitive effects of the combination will be closely scrutinized.

In the case of troubled institutions, special federal provisions have been established for the cross-border acquisitions. The 1982 Garn-St Germain Depository Act permits the interstate acquisition of failed banks with assets of $500 million or more, even if such acquisitions are not consistent with state law. The Competitive Equality Banking Act of 1987 widened the scope of this power to:

- Large institutions that are in danger of closing
- Large bridge banks[8]
- Bank holding companies with one or more banks in danger of closing with aggregate assets of $500 million or more

The 1982 Garn-St Germain Act also permitted the interstate acquisition of failed thrifts and, in some cases, their conversion into banks. The 1989 Financial Institutions Reform, Recovery, and Enforcement Act expanded this power to any thrift with conversions to bank charters under some circumstances.

In recent years, the general regulatory climate with respect to bank mergers and acquisitions generally has been tolerate. No doubt, this tolerance is at least partially attributable to recognition of the inevitability of nationwide banking.

The Interstate Banking Act

The Riegle-Neal Interstate Banking and Branching Efficiency Act of 1994 was passed after many earlier versions of this legislation had been defeated. The major provisions of the act are outlined in Exhibit 1–6.

Exhibit 1–6
Provisions of the Riegle-Neal Interstate Banking and Branching Act of 1994

- Interstate Bank Holding Company Acquisitions
- Interstate Bank Mergers
- *De Novo* Interstate Bank Branching
- Foreign Bank Interstate Branching
- Interstate Bank Agency

Source: Stock, Stuart C. and Peter L. Flanagan. "Riegle-Neal Interstate Banking and Branching Efficiency Act of 1994: Summary."

Interstate Bank Holding Company Acquisitions

Beginning in September 1995, a bank holding company (BHC) may acquire banks located in any state. States may not prohibit or "opt-out" of these interstate BHC acquisitions. However, individual states may establish a minimum age of local banks (up to 5 years) that are subject to interstate acquisition by out-of-state BHCs. (For purposes of this provision, the home state of a BHC is the state in which its banking subsidiaries have the largest amount of deposits as of the later of July 1, 1966, or the date on which the company became a BHC.)

In order to qualify, the acquiring BHC must be adequately capitalized and managed. Even if the BHC is qualified for the acquisition, the Federal Reserve Board (FRB) may not approve the acquisition if:

- After the acquisition, the BHC will control more than 10% of U.S. insured depository institution deposits, or

- The BHC already has a depository institution affiliate in the host state and, after the acquisition, the acquiring BHC will control 30% or more of the insured depository institution deposits of the host state.

Even if the 30% limitation is exceeded, the FRB may approve the acquisition if the host state has established a higher limit. At the same time, a state may limit the share of deposits held within the state by any bank or BHC as long as the limitation does not discriminate against out-of-state banking organizations.

The FRB will also consider the extent of compliance with the CRA. Notwithstanding these stipulations, the act gives the FRB the authority to approve an acquisition if the target bank is in default (or in danger of default) or if the FDIC is providing assistance for the acquisition.

Interstate Bank Mergers

Beginning June, 1997, national and state banks may merge across state lines, thus creating interstate branches. However, such mergers may not take place if the home state of one of the banks has enacted, prior to June 1997, legislation that prohibits or "opts-out" of interstate bank mergers. However, any such law will not affect mergers approved prior to the effective date of the opt-out legislation.

States may "opt-in" prior to June 1997 and also may establish a minimum age (up to 5 years) of local banks that are permitted to participate in interstate mergers. Both home states of the merging banks must have adopted early opt-in legislation. A host state may not discriminate against out-of-state banking organizations in this legislation with the exception of establishing a nation-wide reciprocity rule.

Such mergers can be undertaken by both affiliate banks and independent banks. Mergers may also involve the acquisition of individual branches of a bank, instead of the entire bank, only if the state in which the branches are located permits such acquisitions by statute.

Also applicable in interstate bank mergers are the provisions that are specified in connection with inter-state bank holding company acquisitions:

- 10% and 30% concentration limitations
- Higher limits permitted by state law
- Different limits that do not discriminate against out-of-state banking organizations
- CRA compliance
- Approval of mergers involving a troubled institution

In reviewing potential mergers, the appropriate federal regulators must determine that each participating bank is adequately capitalized and that the resultant bank will be adequately capitalized and well managed. Furthermore, nothing in the act affects the applicability of antitrust laws or the ability of states to charter, supervise, regulate, and examine banks within their state boundaries.

After the merger is complete, the resultant bank may continue to operate those offices that had been in operation prior to the merger. The resultant institution also may acquire additional branches in any location where the acquired bank previously could have established and acquired branches.

The branches of an out-of-state bank will be subject to the host state laws, whether the out-of-state bank has a national charter or a state charter. If the out-of-state bank is a national bank, the Office of the Comptroller will enforce applicable state laws for national banks in the host state. If the out-of-state bank is a state-chartered bank, the branches will be subject to the same laws as other state banks in the host state. However, the branches of an out-of-state state-chartered bank may not engage in any activity not permissible for a bank that is chartered in the host state.

De Novo *Interstate Bank Branching*

A national or state bank may, with appropriate federal approval, establish a *de novo* branch in a state outside its home state in which it previously has not maintained a branch.[9] However, the host state must have enacted legislation that applies to all banks and specifically permits all out-of-state banks to branch de novo into the host state. All state and federal laws that apply to an existing branch also apply to a *de novo* branch.

Foreign Bank Interstate Branching

Essentially, foreign banks are permitted to engage in interstate bank mergers and establish *de novo* interstate branches to the same extent and on the same conditions as national and state banks. However, Federal regulators may require a foreign bank to establish a U.S. subsidiary to branch interstate if the regulators determine that they can verify the foreign bank's compliance with capital adequacy guidelines only through the use of a separate subsidiary. Also, any branch of a foreign bank will continue to be subject to CRA requirements unless the branch receives only deposits that are permissible for an Edge Act Corporation.[10]

Interstate Bank Agency

Beginning one year from enactment of the legislation, a bank may receive deposits, renew time deposits, close loans, service loans, and receive payments on loans and other obligations as agent for any bank or thrift affiliate, whether the affiliate is located in the same state or a different state than the agent bank. However, a depository institution may neither conduct, as agent, an activity that it is prohibited from conducting as a principal, nor have an agent conduct for it any activity that it is prohibited from conducting as principal. Also, if an out-of-state bank is not prohibited from operating a branch in a host state (because of an opt-out statute), a savings institution affiliate located in the host state may act as agent for the bank.

Taken together, the provisions of the Interstate Banking Act provide a framework for a far more efficient banking system in the United States. The industry's consolidation to follow will lead to more convenient access for bank customers, more technological advancements, and better diversification of bank portfolios.

The New Nationwide Banking Environment

As many as 60 million Americans live in metropolitan areas that represent more than one state. It has been estimated that four million people commute across state lines. For these citizens, it will no longer be necessary to maintain multiple bank accounts or to wait several days before their deposits are posted.

However, merging banks must not sacrifice credit availability and customer service. When creditworthiness is evaluated from a central location, character and other more qualitative factors can be overlooked. If higher bank fees are charged in a community because a new parent bank routinely charges higher fees in other markets, the consuming public will be disadvantaged.

At the same time, merging banks will realize substantial diversification and efficiency benefits. If banks had been permitted to operate nationwide, perhaps the economic crises in the Northeast and Southwest would not have devastated the banking systems in these regions. Also, larger banks can lower their cost of funds, service credit cards more efficiently, offer better mortgage services, market their services more effectively, and streamline administrative costs.

The challenge for banks in an environment of nationwide banking will be to select the right merger partners, examining all aspects of product mix, customer base, and systems integration.

Selected References

Federal Deposit Insurance Corporation. "FDIC Statement of Policy: Bank Merger Transactions," Washington, D.C.: author, December 31, 1989.

Fitch, Thomas. *Dictionary of Banking Terms*, Hauppauge, New York: Barron's Educational Series, Inc., 1990.

Holland, Kelley. "A Delicate Balance at the Bank," *Business Week*, January 9, 1995.

Hylton, Richard D. "Can Banks Make It On Wall Street?" *Fortune*, October 31, 1994, pp. 199–202.

Johnson, Hazel J. *Financial Institutions and Markets: A Global Perspective*, New York: McGraw-Hill, 1993.

Knecht, G. Bruce. "Nationwide Banking Is Around the Corner, But Obstacles Remain," *Wall Street Journal*, July 26, 1994, pp. A1 & A8.

LaWare, John P. Member, Board of Governors of the Federal Reserve System; Statement Before the Committee on Banking, Housing and Urban Affairs; United States Senate, October 5, 1993.

Lohse, Deborah. "Interstate Banking Promises Conveniences—And Costs," *Wall Street Journal*, August 3, 1994, pp. C1 & C11.

NationsBank Corporation. NationsBank News Release, Charlotte, NC, September 13, 1994.

NationsBank Corporation. "Redefining Banking—Who, What, When, Where, and How: The Vision for NationsBank in the Era of Interstate Banking," NationsBank Speakers Resource, Charlotte, NC.

Spong, Kenneth. *Banking Regulation: Its Purposes, Implementation, and Effects*, 3e, Kansas City: Federal Reserve Bank of Kansas City, 1990.

Stock, Stuart C. and Peter L. Flanagan. "Riegle-Neal Interstate Banking and Branching Efficiency Act of 1994: Summary," Washington, D.C.: Covington & Burling, September 16, 1994 (Through the Legal Division of the Board of Governors of the Federal Reserve System, Washington, D.C.).

Endnotes

1 NationsBank News Release, September 13, 1994.

2 Depository institutions are commercial banks, savings and loan associations, mutual savings banks, and credit unions.

3 See Richard D. Hylton, "Can Banks Make It On Wall Street?"

4 See NationsBank, "Redefining Banking—Who, What, When, Where, and How."

5 The 19 multistate banking organizations in existence in 1956 were grandfathered when the Bank Holding Company Act was passed. Most of these were small, with four holding 86% of the assets of the 19 institutions.

6 The regulatory bodies that are appropriate for state banks are state banking authorities, the Federal Reserve System (if they are members), and the Federal Deposit Insurance Corporation (if they are nonmember, insured banks). The Comptroller of the Currency is primarily responsible for national banks. The Federal Reserve is the primary federal regulator for bank holding companies.

7 As applicable, regulators also expect full compliance with the National Environmental Act and the National Historic Preservation Act.

8 A bridge bank is a national bank organized to assume the deposits and secured liabilities of an insolvent bank. FDIC is permitted to charter these institutions by the Competitive Equality Banking Act and may operate a bridge bank for up to 3 years until a buyer is found.

9 A *de novo* bank or branch is a newly chartered bank or branch, as opposed to an existing office acquired through acquisition.

10 An Edge Act Corporation is chartered by the Federal Reserve, owned by state or national banks, may operate interstate branches, accepts deposits outside the United States, and invests in non-U.S. firms. The Edge Act subsidiary buys and sells notes, drafts, and bills of exchange, complimenting the international banking activities of the parent bank.

2

Bank Mergers

Introduction

A merger is a combination of two or more organizations through pooling of common stock, cash payment to the bank being acquired, or a combination of the two. In bank mergers, the managements of the two institutions typically consent.[1] Bank CEOs are continuously discussing the next potential merger partner, with many questions surrounding this issue.

- When is the right time to merge?
- How do you identify the right partner?
- How do you successfully communicate the benefits of the merger to market analysts?
- How do you approach consolidating the two banks?

The Right Time to Merge

Not long ago, banks competed primarily through their branch network locations. It was not uncommon for a commercial bank to seek to grow by 10% to 15% per year. If this goal could not be accomplished by attracting more business to the existing banking offices, then often it could be done by merging with other institutions. During the 1970s, this growth was considered the key to banking "success." Profitability was not a real issue because the bank's interest rate spread was assured via regulated interest rates.

Today, bank profits are not automatically assured. There is keen competition and, in some cases, margins are razor-thin. Each institution must decide exactly how it will carve out its niche(s)—credit cards, automobile loans, mortgage banking, high-technology applications (such as extensive ATM networks and home banking), small business finance, the corporate middle market, wholesale banking, or trade finance. To this list, larger institutions may add investment banking and derivatives.

In order to assess the right time to merge, each institution must identify its strategic direction after thoroughly analyzing its strengths, weaknesses, opportunities, and threats (SWOT). The process contains the elements noted in Exhibit 2–1:

Exhibit 2–1

The Foundation for Deciding the Right Time to Merge

- The Bank's Mission
- Bank Industry Analysis
- Analysis of Strengths, Weaknesses, Opportunities, and Threats
- The Bank's Strategic Plan

- Defining the bank's mission
- Performing an industry analysis
- Conducting a SWOT analysis
- Crafting a strategic plan

A bank's *mission statement* defines the institution's overall reason for being, its role in the community in which it operates, and perhaps its style of management. This statement is typically a two- to three-paragraph document that reflects the culture of the institution and its focus. The two overriding questions that the mission statement will answer are: "Who are we?" and "Why are we here?" The mission statement is necessarily concise because it must capture sentiments that can be shared by every employee of the bank.

The purpose of the *industry analysis* is to survey the banking industry and the direction of future trends. An industry analysis should incorporate the competitive forces from within and outside of the commercial banking community. Factors will include:

- The demographics of the banking community served
- The impact of technology on the delivery of banking services, including payment mechanisms and credit
- Future efficiencies that will likely be achieved in the processing of bank transactions
- The likely impact of nationwide banking on the local banking community
- National trends in banking
- The nonbank alternatives to traditional banking services

- An evaluation of the general economic
  climate from a short-, medium-, and
  long-term perspective
- The direction of regulatory oversight

While many of these analyses are clearly subjective, it is vital to have a hearing and synthesis of the perceptions of management as to the environment in which the bank is operating.

The next step is to conduct a *SWOT analysis.* This requires a totally candid view of the bank. Strengths, weaknesses, opportunities, and threats should be assessed by all management employees, with input from the staff. This list of attributes in each case should be as exhaustive as possible, consider present and future market conditions, and include competitive factors related to all providers of financial services.

The last step in this process is to craft a *strategic plan.* This plan will incorporate the results of the three prior steps to outline:

- Overarching goals
- Specific strategies to achieve these goals

The time frame covered by the strategic plan should be at least five years with intermediate milestones specified. While goals are general in nature, strategies are more specific.

The following are examples of goals and strategies that might accompany them:

Goal #1:   *To become one of the most efficient bank-*
                   ing institutions in the region.
Strategy 1–1:   Increase deposit and loan account fee

income by 50% within three years and
by 100% within five years.

Strategy 1–2: Increase operating expense by no
more than 25% for the next three years
and by no more than 50% over the
next five years.

Goal #2: *To become one of the strongest marketers
of mutual funds in the region within five
years.*

Strategy 2–1: Within one year, redesign the work
flow pattern to facilitate the cross-selling of bank products by all bank representatives with client contact.

Strategy 2–2: Within one year, restructure the
bank's offerings of mutual funds to
include a full range of money market,
bond, equity, and international fund
offerings.

Strategy 2–3: Within four years, develop a propri-
etary line of mutual funds to complement the third-party mutual funds
offered.

Strategy 2–4: Increase fees from mutual fund business to 200% of current fees within
three years and to 500% of current fees
within five years.

Both these examples of goals and strategies suggest a
need for future growth by the bank—the first, growth in
deposit and loan fee income, the second, growth in investment product fee income. If the bank's management deter-
mines that these strategies cannot reasonably be realized

in the context of the current organization, it may be the right time to consider a merger with a bank with attributes that will compliment this growth initiative. Likewise, if it appears that containing costs in the current organization may be difficult while still growing fee income, it may be an appropriate time to consider merging with another bank in the area (in-market merger) to reduce operating cost while maintaining an equivalent level of service.

In essence, the right time to merge will depend on the bank's view of its position in the market, its strengths and weaknesses, and its future direction. If there are elements of the strategic plan that may be accomplished best by combining with another institution, then it is the right time to merge.

The Right Merger Partner

Within the context of a bank's strategic plan, the right merger partner will offer the bank one or more of the following attributes:

- Loan portfolio diversification
- Cost reductions on a per-dollar-of-assets basis
- Geographic expansion
- Expertise in an area of financial services that has been targeted through the strategic plan

An analysis of a potential merger partner should consider a number of aspects, including the institution itself, its products and strategies, market position, customers, costs, organization, ownership, legal and environmental considerations, human resource management, and culture (Exhibit 2–2). The following is an example of the points that should be covered in this analysis.

Description of the merger candidate:

- Short history of the development and performance of the bank
- Main lines of business and location of branch network
- Size of the bank
- Description of the balance sheet ratios with respect to lending vs. securities investment, deposits vs. short-term borrowings vs. long-term debt, use of leverage
- Management of the bank, including extent of experience, depth of qualified management
- Main strengths and weaknesses
- Relationships with regulatory agencies

Exhibit 2–2

Factors to Consider in Identifying the Right Merger Partner

- Size, History, and Status
- Main Products and Strategies
- Geographic Location and Market Share
- Client/Customer Base
- Operational and Financial Costs
- Quality of Management
- Nature of Ownership
- Legal Status
- Human Resources Profile
- Corporate Culture and Decision Making Process

- Previous mergers with other institutions and the experiences associated with those mergers

Main products and strategies of the merger candidate:

- Product mix, including assets, liabilities, and off-balance sheet categories
- History of successful and unsuccessful product development
- Line of business profitability
- Perception of quality of banking services offered by merger candidate
- Potential new banking products being considered
- Strength of the banking franchise of the merger candidate

Market position of the merger candidate:

- Geographic markets served by the candidate
- Market share controlled by the candidate
- Image and reputation within the industry
- Likely changes in the market position of the merger candidate

Customers of the merger candidate:

- Main clientele groups of the candidate
- Current banking needs of the clientele
- Changing banking needs of the clientele
- The image and reputation of the candidate among its clientele
- Impact of a merger on the clientele

Cost Configuration:

- Operational efficiency, including check processing and loan payments processing
- Condition of operational systems
- Extent of use of technology within operational systems
- Cost of funds, including deposits and borrowed funds
- Salaries expense as a percentage of interest and fee income

Specific organization and management of the merger candidate:

- Formal organization chart
- "Informal" organization, including powerful members of the central decision-making team
- Board of directors
- Backgrounds and competencies of the key managers
- Apparent motivation of the key managers in terms of career goals and realized advancement to-date
- Compensation packages of key managers

Ownership of the merger candidate:

- Is ownership closely or widely held?
- Who are the shareholders?
- How is control of the candidate exercised?
- Shareholder voting arrangements
- Warrants, rights, and/or stock options outstanding

- Which shareholders want to sell their stock?
- Why do these shareholders want to sell?

Legal and environment considerations:

- Where is the merger candidate incorporated?
- Where does the stock trade?
- Are there mortgage obligations or other liens that could affect the sale of assets?
- Are there significant unfunded pension and/or medical retirement benefits?
- Are there any active lawsuits involving the candidate?
- Are there any other contracts or informal obligations that should be taken into consideration?
- Are there any environmental issues that affect the operation of the candidate?
- Does the candidate have adequate insurance— both property/casualty and errors/omissions?

Human resource management of the merger candidate:

- What are the strengths and weaknesses of the management team?
- What are the skills and capabilities of the bank staff?
- Do the employees of the merger candidate appear to be well motivated?
- Do the employees appear to identify with the current owner(s) and management team?
- What is the breakdown of employees and managers by job classification?

- What are the salary levels of these job classifications and are they comparable to the industry?
- What is the age and seniority of the bank staff and management team?
- What level of education does the bank staff have?
- What is the extent of employee turnover by job classification and how does it compare with the industry average?
- What provisions exist for overtime work, part-time employees, and temporary employees?
- What are the description and cost of the existing package of fringe benefits, including vacation, health care, profit-sharing, stock purchase plans?
- How do these provisions compare with those of the bank performing the analysis?

Corporate culture of the merger candidate:

- What is the candidate's management style?
- What is the nature of the "group spirit?"
- Are decisions made centrally or are many decisions made at the work-group level?
- How are the functions of the bank organized—lending, deposit services, retail vs. corporate banking?
- What is the relative power of these functional areas with respect to decision making?
- What is the philosophy of management with respect to expansion, organizational planning,

future banking trends, product development, marketing, financing, and dividend payments to shareholders?
* Are the philosophies of the merger candidate comparable with those of the bank performing the analysis?

These points can be helpful in constructing an objective framework in which to measure the appropriateness of pursuing merger discussions with a potential candidate. The objective is not only to identify an organization with characteristics that are comparable to those of the bank performing the analysis, but also to identify those institutions that have competencies that will complement and facilitate the realization of organizational goals and strategies.

Communicating Merger Benefits to Market Analysts

Once managers and directors of two banks have concluded merger negotiations, all other interested parties must then be convinced of the wisdom of the combination. This communication will occur at several levels:

* Employee communications
* Shareholder communications
* Press communications/press releases
* Professional market analyst briefings

The timing of these communications is critical. Employees should be first to learn, followed shortly by shareholders, and then the media. It is vital that employees and shareholders not learn of a merger from the media. Such a sequence will lead almost certainly to feelings of disenfranchisement and alienation—subsequently leading to difficulties in consolidating the two entities. At the same time, leaking information about the merger too far in advance will encourage illegal speculation in the stock market based on insider information.[2]

The key element in this communication is that value will be added to the institutions involved in the merger. The information that should be communicated includes:

- The nature of the agreement, the size of the resulting institution, and the resulting ranking of the new institution either nationally or regionally.
- The geographic market that the combined organization will service.
- The new name of the organization and its headquarters.
- The officers of the new organization and the composition of the new board of directors.
- The compensation to shareholders, both stock and cash, as applicable.
- If shareholders have an option of receiving stock or cash, the date by which this election must be made.
- The market value of the merger at current stock prices.
- Whether the merger has any immediate dilutive effects on the stock of either institution.
- The long-term benefits of the merger in terms of shareholders and the banking community that it serves.

- Any cost reduction plans and how such cost reduction will increase shareholder wealth.
- The anticipated time frame over which the cost reductions will be completed.
- How the two organizations will complement each other in terms of relative strengths and weaknesses.
- How the merger will better position the institution for long-term viability.
- The strategic focus of the new organization.
- Any further approvals that are necessary, such as shareholder approval of both institutions, state banking officials, and federal regulatory agencies.
- The date by which any further approvals are expected to be received.
- Stock market listing of the stock of the new bank and the anticipated level of dividend payments.
- The investment bankers that have been involved in the merger.
- The opinions of these investment bankers with respect to stock valuation and exchange ratios of the stock of the respective banks.
- Selected pro forma financial information about the individual and merged institutions, including securities, loans, assets, deposits, equity, net income, return on assets, return on equity, debt-to-equity ratios, number of offices, number of cities in which offices are located, number of shareholders, and number of employees.

This information should be contained in any press release provided for general media purposes at the time of merger announcement.

The communication of the details of the merger is the first critical step in introducing the merger to all concerned parties. However, it must be followed by in-house information sessions with employees, including question-and-answer periods. These Q-and-A sessions will help to clarify any questions not directly addressed by the information provided by management. Such sessions play an important role in assuring employees that management is committed to keeping the staff fully apprised of the status and progress of the merger. In other words, the communication of all relevant information is a vital exercise in "full disclosure" to the employees, who must have a sense of trust in the process in order for the new institution to realize the anticipated benefits of merging.

In addition, broadcast and print media advertising should be undertaken to convey to banking customers (1) the culture of the new banking institution, (2) the banking philosophy of the new institution, and (3) the improvement in services that they can anticipate. These communications will help ensure customer loyalty and a general attitude of open-mindedness to the change. This is particularly true for an institution whose name will change.

An on-going media campaign for financial market analysts should not be overlooked. All mergers are completed by swapping stock to at least some extent. Most involve the exchange of stock at some predetermined exchange ratio. The value of the stock to be exchanged and, thus the value of the merger to shareholders, will be based on the perception of the stock market with respect to the wisdom and effectiveness of the merger. The perception of the stock market will be filtered through stock market analysts. The bank's communication with these analysts should be given top priority. Poor communications not only can affect shareholder wealth in the context of a merger currently being undertaken, but can also hurt the prospects for future mergers that will be based on stock swaps. (See Exhibit 2–3.)

Effective communication of the process and benefits of merging will have many positive effects. Shareholders will be less likely to challenge the merger, employees will be more receptive to change, and market analysts will have reasonable expectations of the future performance of the merged institution.

Exhibit 2–3
The Golden Rules of Communicating
the Benefits of the Merger

- Communicate to employees, shareholders, the media, and financial market analysts.
- Communicate increased value and enhanced service.
- Communicate early.
- Communicate frequently.
- Communicate honestly.
- Communicate the resolution of uncertainty.

Consolidating the Two Banks

Careful and thoughtful communication of merger plans must be followed by equally well planned implementation of the merger. To be most effective, the implementation plan (at least a blueprint for the implementation plan) should have been drafted prior to merger announcement. If this is not the case, the transition can move very slowly and the strategic and economic value of the merger can be lost, delaying and perhaps reducing shareholder value effects of combining the two institutions.

The implementation plan should include a transition team that is composed of executives from each institution. Each functional area should also have a specific plan for consolidation with projected completion dates for key elements of the transition. There are a number of important caveats with respect to merger implementation:

- Recognize that a merger consolidation is a rapid, traumatic change that redefines all operations.
- Recognize that the longer the consolidation takes, the more likely it is that customers will be lost, new product offerings will not materialize, key employees will resign, and competing financial institutions will take advantage of what appears to be chaos or, at least, indecisiveness.
- Avoid assembling a transition team that is too large to coordinate meeting schedules effectively or make decisions in a timely fashion.
- Make a commitment to keep the lines of communication open during the implementation

phase, sharing both realized goals and unanticipated problems.

- Move quickly to resolve the sensitive issues that are most likely to create animosity and derail the consolidation process—salaries, titles, positions, and other issues related to personal opportunity and security.
- Recognize that each management team will have vested interests in maintaining its own procedures or, at a minimum, probably will believe that its procedures are "best practice."
- Be prepared to redesign procedures to achieve the best results for the new organization.

In a merger of equals, the two institutions are presumed to have equivalent power to make decisions within the consolidated entity. Expectations of such even-handed control can be frustrated, however, unless both parties in the merger recognize that their autonomy will be constrained by the compromises which necessarily accompany any business combination.

Practices and Procedures

In evaluating the practices that will be adopted by the new institution, the transition team should be prepared to examine each functional area objectively. This process should be geared to creating efficiencies in operating expense while still maintaining high-quality service. For example, consider the mortgage function. The application process for mortgage loans for both institutions should be analyzed to determine efficiency in terms of the quality of customer information obtained, the convenience for mortgage applicants, and the time required to obtain an approval. The application process that is adopted for the combined institution should be redefined to incorporate the most efficient elements of the two existing systems and any modifications that would improve the process further.

In every case, quality control should be stressed. The most efficient operation will spend the least amount of time correcting errors. Time spent undoing tasks that have been improperly executed is time wasted and can lead to actual losses to the bank. This is true in the areas of operations (check clearing and ATM transactions), loan portfolio management (credit standards, diversification, market environment, and client relationships), and customer service (competitive rates and product lines).

Operational Systems

Systems integration can take place after the "best practice" approach has been identified in each area. There is no single best approach to this integration process. However, generally, there are three ways that systems integration can be accomplished:

- One bank can adopt totally the systems of the other.
- The two banks can maintain separate systems.
- The two banks can mix the best of both systems, for example, using the loan system of one and the deposit system of the other.

The circumstance under which one bank would adopt the systems of the other is more often appropriate in the case of the combination of a large institution with a considerably smaller institution. Such a combination is more often characterized as an acquisition rather than a merger. The "absorption" of one system by another is fast and generates the greatest savings among the three alternatives. The greatest economies of scale are possible through this alternative, extensive consolidation of back office systems is possible, the operation of only one of the two banks is affected, and the actual cost of conversion is minimized. However, this approach can create dissension among the managers of the bank doing the conversion and the identity of the converting may be lost.

Maintaining separate systems may be the correct alternative if the two institutions are in different and distant locations. Clearly, modifying systems can be time-consuming and expensive. Maintaining separate systems encourages autonomous operation, helps preserve the identity of both institutions, and avoids the necessity to (and the cost of) terminating existing system contracts. However, the degree of long-term cost savings associated with maintaining separate systems is limited. There are no economies of scale, back-office consolidation is not possible, and the banks appear to be two different institutions.

The third alternative of selecting among the systems for the "best practice" system in each area takes considerably more time and can become a political process if each management team fights to maintain its systems. This alternative is also more expensive than the other two alternatives because the systems of both institutions change. However, this approach emphasizes the equality of the partners in the merger, allows the banks to appear as one institution to its customers, and results in the best possible systems.

In some cases, the systems of one of the two banks may be in considerable need of modernization. Such an example might be a five-bank holding company that has five different DDA systems and software applications that have not been updated for over 10 years. Obviously, correcting such deficiencies can be expensive. Accordingly, it is extremely important that the review of operational systems be initiated immediately upon commencement of merger talks.[3]

Building Working Relationships

At the heart of consolidation of the two institutions is the ability to communicate among the transition team, management teams, and bank staffs. In turn, the ability to communicate will depend to a large extent on the perceptions of these individuals and their shared perceptions. While managers may feel that managing perceptions is less significant than the other pressing issues surrounding a merger, these tendencies must be resisted. Subtle, but important, actions can vastly improve the comfort level and effectiveness of working relationships.

Managers can build credibility by perceived truthfulness of communication, demonstration of personal competence and fairness, and delivery of resources to accomplish the specified target outcomes. The early statements with respect to the merger and its effects must be perceived as true and followed by appropriate actions. When managers provide real assistance in the transition process and perform as promised, the trust of the bank staff and other members of the management team is strengthened. This trust helps to increase the likelihood that the best employees will be encouraged to stay and that low morale will not hamper the progress of the merger.

The Decision to Sell the Bank

In some cases, a review of the strengths and weaknesses of a bank leads its directors to the conclusion that the best way to maximize the value of shareholder wealth is for the bank to be merged with another institution. This may be attributable to the relative illiquidity of the bank's stock. Or the decision may be more related to the regulatory environment. The increased cost of regulation for a small bank is more difficult to offset if that bank does not have significant growth potential on its own.

The managers of small banks often grapple with the issue of how they can provide more value for their shareholders. For example, in 1993, the $102-million Rio Salado Bancorp in Tempe, Arizona, considered raising capital to support growth. The shares were selling at book value and this would probably not change without some growth in the scale of operations. After hiring an outside consultant, however, the decision was made to slow the growth in its loan portfolio and to emphasize fee income from mortgage banking, annuities, and mutual funds. This approach would not dilute the existing shareholders' wealth but would boost the bank's bottom line. At that point, there was no intention to merge, despite the fact that there would still be no active market in the stock.

Early in 1994, the CEO of Rio Salado received a telephone call from Zion Bancorp in Utah. As it turned out, the call was an offer that Rio Salado could not refuse. The offer was for two-and-a-half times book value. Furthermore, when Rio Salado merged with Zion Bancorp, the Rio Salado shareholders held marketable stock that represented four times the value of their original investment. And the bank's customers also derived benefits from the merger, as the new bank has higher lending limits and offers a wider range of services.

Generally, healthy institutions can expect to be approached about the prospect of selling the bank. In many cases, the bank being approached has little experience with mergers. (In some cases, the bank that suggests merger discussions also has little experience.) It is better to consider the issue *before* being approached to avoid making ill-advised decisions. Should the bank sell or remain independent? The answer to this question should be driven by the same process that supports the decision to seek merger partners: an established mission, an objective assessment of the bank in the context of industry trends, and a strategic plan.

However, once an unsolicited bid has been received, the bank's directors first must decide whether to respond to the offer. If there is no genuine interest to pursue a merger, generally no response is required.[4] However, if there is genuine interest (as opposed to simple curiosity), the directors of the bank must consider several factors:

- The origin and impact of the offer
- The process of evaluating the offer
- The attractiveness of the offer

Questions with respect to the *origin and impact of the offer* center around the bidder and the consequences of selling the bank under terms of the offer. Does the bidder have substantial business background and a long-term strategic plan that is consistent with the current offer? These considerations speak to the issues of whether the shareholders initially will perceive the offer as a serious one and, likewise, whether the bidder has serious intentions.

Also, has the bidder provided evidence that the deal can be financed if cash or debt is to be used? What impact would this financing have on the bank? A highly leveraged transaction will have more wealth shifting characteristics than a more straightforward equity exchange. In such a case, the shareholders of the bidder may realize a substantial profit by using debt financing to acquire control of the bank and selling bank assets to repay some portion of the debt, gaining control of the bank with relatively little investment. In the meantime, bank's current shareholders may be forced to exchange equity for riskier debt securities with uncertain market characteristics and little or no potential for capital appreciation.

Also important are the plans of the bidder relative to treatment of employees and management of the bank. Will some or all of the employees be retained? What will be the roles and designations of the bank's managers? Will the board of directors continue to exist after the merger? What will be the new corporate name of the bank?

With respect to *evaluating the offer*, there are several basic issues to be addressed to ensure sound decision making and to avoid subsequent legal actions against the board of directors by shareholders dissatisfied with decisions of the board.

- What written information has the board received concerning the offer? To begin the evaluation process, the directors must have complete, reliable information about the offer itself.

- How much time does the board have to respond? A timetable for evaluating the offer must provide the directors adequate time to (1) individually consider the offer and (2) collectively discuss the issues to arrive at a decision or counteroffer.
- Does the board understand its legal obligations? The directors should have a written legal opinion as to their duties from experienced, independent counsel. This opinion should include a description of all laws that apply to directors in the home state of the bank.
- What support do the directors have in the evaluation process? The board should have the input of bank consultants, investment bankers, attorneys, and accountants. In this way, the directors will be able to assess the implications of the merger from all relevant perspectives— banking, financial, legal, and accounting.
- Does management of the bank have the technical expertise to evaluate and negotiate the offer? Since a merger has major implications with respect to all obligations of the bank, management must also be able to provide input to the decision-making process. A negotiation team should have representation from all functional areas of the bank and have clearly defined duties, goals, and strategies.
- Has the process of documenting the decision-making process been determined? It is not sufficient to conduct a well-planned, comprehensive review of the merger offer. The board

of directors must be able to demonstrate and document that this process has occurred. This documentation must provide evidence of the board's caution, diligence, and competence.

In terms of the *attractiveness of the offer*, the board must consider the structure of the deal. Are the financial terms generally attractive? Is the deal legal and feasible? What will be the total effect of the merger on the bank and its shareholders?

If the answer to one or more of these questions is "no," the board has the obligation to identify alternatives for purposes of a counteroffer. Also, the board must consider the legal status of the bidder with respect to lawsuits or regulatory problems that could prevent the bidder from completing the merger as specified.

The consideration of these issues places substantial responsibility on the bank's board of directors. These responsibilities may also be affected by other regulatory requirements. For example, some states permit corporations to include in their articles of incorporation a requirement that directors consider the interests of parties other than stockholders in mergers and acquisitions. Some federal laws specifically require the consideration of other parties. For example, the Community Reinvestment Act and the Riegle-Neal Interstate Banking and Branch Act make special provisions for the consideration of customers in low-income areas when mergers are being considered.

Beyond the Price

The decision to merge or to be merged has implications far beyond the price paid. It is not a decision made in isolation, nor should it be a decision made in haste. Once the decision to merge is made, the right merger partner is the key to success. Proper planning, open communications, and decisive action after the merger announcement will ensure the success of the combined institution.

Selected References

Cocheo, Steve. "Big Mergers Aren't the Only Action," *ABA Banking Journal*, February 1994, pp. 46–50.

Goldstein, Jerry. "Integrating Strategic Planning and Marketing," *The Bankers' Handbook*, 3e, Homewood, Illinois: Dow Jones-Irwin, 1988.

Haspeslagh, Philippe C. and David B. Jemison. *Managing Acquisitions: Creating Value Through Corporate Renewal*, New York: The Free Press, 1991.

Huggins, Stanley M. "They Want to Buy Your Bank. Now What?" *ABA Banking Journal*, May 1994, pp. 54–58.

Radding, Alan. "Systems Integration Is Often the Key to Successful Mergers," *Bank Management*, April 1993, pp. 60–63.

Rock, Milton L., Robert H. Rock, and Martin Sikora. *The Mergers & Acquisitions Handbook*, 2e, New York: McGraw-Hill, Inc., 1994.

Rosenberg, Richard M. "Success Components for the 21st Century," *Bank Management*, January/February 1994, pp. 32–38.

Endnotes

1   In the case of a failed institution, the approval of the appropriate regulatory bodies is required.

2   Trading in takeover stocks with the expectation of making a profit using undisclosed, market-sensitive information is referred to as *misappropriation* of nonpublic information by the Securities and Exchange Commission and is prohibited by SEC Rule 10b–5. Officers, directors, and other corporate officials owning at least 10% of the bank's stock must report trades to the SEC.

3   See the discussion of cost configuration in the section above entitled "The Right Merger Partner."

4   If there is no interest and the directors respond, they risk unnecessarily encouraging the bidder, eliciting a stronger offer from the bidder, market rumors that lead to speculation in the stock, and needlessly raising concerns by shareholders and employees about the future of the bank.

3

Bank Acquisitions

Introduction

A merger is called an acquisition when one of the banks in the transaction, usually the larger, takes over the other institution and consolidates the two organizations into a single entity. The acquirer's name is usually retained and control of the decision-making process rests almost entirely with the acquirer. This form of bank combination has been particularly important as regional agreements have permitted banks in many states to expand by acquiring banks across state lines.[1] Another example of an acquisition in the banking industry is the absorption of a smaller firm in a different industry that complements banking and helps the acquirer diversify its services. This activity will be heightened at such time as the Glass-Steagall Act is modified or repealed.[2] The ability to offer more services in the securities field will accelerate the pace of acquisitions by well-capitalized regional institutions.

Acquisition Guidelines

The process of increasing a commercial bank's market share through acquisitions should begin with the same process that drives bank mergers. A well-conceived strategic plan will serve as guidance in terms of timing and appropriate acquisition target(s). (See Chapter 2, sections entitled "The Right Time to Merge" and "The Right Merger Partner.") Additional guidelines in a successful acquisition program involve:

- Assembling the right acquisition team
- Narrowing the field of acquisition targets
- Designing strategies to approach the acquisition target
- Deciding on the use of brokers and finders

The Acquisition Team

The managers and outside consultants that are members of the acquisition team will reflect the competencies that are required to effectively negotiate with and integrate the acquisition target. The team should include legal experts, accountants or lawyers that are familiar with tax law, finance professionals, and investment bankers.

The *legal experts* will provide important input with respect to the aspects of the transaction that relate to taking over a public corporation. These members of the team will be responsible for the review of applicable state and federal securities laws, the antitrust considerations (market concentration, for example), necessary regulatory approvals, and the legal implications of alternative acquisition strategies. If the acquisition target is not a publicly traded corporation, internal counsel of the acquiring bank may be able to provide guidance in the legal issues involved in the acquisition. Even if the internal legal staff is competent in the matters involved with the acquisition, retaining outside counsel can enhance the effectiveness and speed with which the acquisition is completed.

The involvement of *accountants or lawyers that are familiar with tax law* is necessary in order to structure the most tax-effective deal. The tax specialists should review the various tax structures that are available for the acquisition and run scenarios analyses based on relevant tax considerations. In this way, the best alternative from a tax perspective can be identified. The scenario analyses should consider the impact of the acquisition on all classes of shareholders—individual, corporate, and trust. Even if the most efficient tax structure is not possible, the analysis can measure the opportunity cost of the tax structure that is adopted. Also, the tax members of the team can determine whether it is necessary to obtain an IRS tax ruling. If the seller requires a tax ruling, the time frame of the transaction must accommodate this process.

The input of *finance professionals* must be included at the early stages of the acquisition analysis to provide input with respect to the value of the acquisition target and the economic impact of the combination. Relevant issues include whether the transaction should be cash vs. a stock swap and whether special provisions are necessary as to the value of stock to be exchanged (for example, provisions in the event of significant declines in market value of the acquirer's stock). The finance professionals should also evaluate the impact of purchase vs. pooling accounting for the transaction. In addition, the finance professionals should evaluate the composition of the acquiree's balance sheet, including:

- Fixed and variable rate instruments
- Duration considerations
- Core deposit base
- Extent of money market financing (short-term borrowed funds)
- Productivity of branches
- Overlap of branches of the acquiring bank and the acquisition target

In essence the finance professionals give the most comprehensive view of the new combined institution after the transaction is complete.

Investment bankers are essential for transactions of all sizes if the acquisition target is a public firm. An investment banker should also be part of the team if the transaction involves a larger firm that is privately held. In selecting an investment banking firm, the employees of the acquiring bank (that are a part of the acquisition team) should meet with the representative(s) of the investment bank to assess the ability of the firm to handle the transaction and their familiarity with similar transactions. Once the selection is made, the acquiring bank should document the selection in a formal engagement letter. These professionals should be involved in all aspects of the acquisition, providing advice on acquisition strategies, high-level access to target management, fairness opinions with respect to valuation, deal structuring, financial advice, and tactics during implementation of the acquisition.

Narrowing the Field of Acquisition Targets

Guidelines for the identification of potential acquisition targets should be based on the strategic plan for the acquiring bank. Given the large number of firms in the banking industry, the identification process should involve all members of the acquisition team. When assembling a preliminary list of banks, the extent of availability should be kept in mind. The probability of a successful acquisition will be increased if the bank in question has been a recent takeover target in a deal that was not completed, is the subject of takeover rumors, has undergone recent substantial top management changes, or appears to be receptive to acquisition for other reasons. The sources of possible candidates include the internal and external members of the acquisition team, the financial or business press, market analysts, and business and personal acquaintances. Of course, if the acquiring bank has a specific geographic market in mind, the preliminary list may include all banks in that geographic region.

If the acquiring bank has access to a data base of commercial banks, the preliminary list of acquisition candidates can include those identified through a parameter search. A *parameter search* involves constructing a model of the institution that is sought using variables that describe location, size, profitability, asset mix, income mix (interest vs. noninterest income), and other variables. For example, using the first parameter, the data base is searched for those banks that satisfy the location parameters. The list of these banks is then reduced to those that satisfy the size parameters. This process continues until all parameters have been introduced.

Once the preliminary list of potential acquisition candidates has been created, the next step is to conduct a full review of the candidates on list with publicly available information. This review includes:

- Apparent availability for acquisition
- Financial analysis
- Market share
- Client base
- Market dynamics (both banks and nonbanks)
- Hidden assets (for example, understated real estate values)
- Hidden liabilities (for example, unfunded pension plans)
- Any significant regulatory issues (that potentially could block the acquisition)

If a particular candidate passes through these filters, the next step is to consider the approach for extending an offer. The approach will depend not only on the objective factors already identified. It will also depend on more subjective, motivational issues with respect to the target bank:

- Do the owners want to sell?
- Is there an apparent problem with management succession?
- Have the directors of the bank strongly disagreed on important issues?
- How much stock do the managers own?
- Have the managers and directors been selling or buying stock?

The answers to these questions will help the acquisition team to structure a deal that has the highest probability of acceptance.

Approaching the Acquisition Target

In general, there are three ways an acquiring firm can approach a target firm:

- Friendly persuasion approach
- Opportunistic approach
- Completely unnegotiated approach

The *friendly persuasion approach* is one in which the acquiring firm attempts to convince the target to negotiate its sale. The advantages of this approach are that it is likely to be the least expensive in terms of time and legal expense, management of the target firm is more likely to remain with the firm, and the acquiring firm will have access to more and better information about the target firm. The acquiring bank will succeed with this approach to the extent that:

- Directors and managers do not have a strong propensity to remain independent.
- The chief executive of the acquiring bank has or can establish good rapport with the chief executive of the acquisition candidate.
- The price that is being offered appears attractive.

In the friendly persuasion approach, it should be remembered that the chief executive of the target firm probably has little incentive to sell. Also, the chief executive will be vitally concerned about the confidentiality of the discussions, lest rumors drive market dynamics to force a sale of the firm.

Opportunistic approaches take advantage of a situation in which the acquisition target (1) has already been targeted by another, unfriendly firm that is attempting an acquisition, (2) has communicated its availability for sale through a broad solicitation being managed by an intermediary (often an investment bank), or (3) has agreed to be sold to another firm.

If the acquisition target is subject to a hostile takeover from a third firm, the acquiring firm can act as a "white knight," that is, a friendly potential buyer, by communicating early on its interest in pursuing acquisition discussions. Even if the takeover attempt has progressed into a full-fledged battle with the third firm, it may be possible for the acquiring firm to enter as a "grey knight," with an attractive offer before a deal is finalized.

In the second case, it is possible that a broad solicitation for sale, even one that is to be associated with an auction, may be converted into a friendly persuasion approach by preempting the auction phase and transforming the process into a one-to-one negotiation. Given time constraints, however, the acquiring firm must be extremely responsive to the seller's price and nonprice objectives, be willing to work virtually around the clock, retain competent advisers to work on the offer, and perform whatever tasks are necessary to complete the deal.

An acquisition under the third condition is referred to as a "swipe" and involves offering a higher price than that which has been accepted by the board of directors. The swipe is most often employed in the case of management-led buy-outs. In these cases, outside directors may have felt the pressure of potential conflicts of interest associated with an insider acquisition and perhaps even an associated low price for the firm.

Completely unnegotiated approaches are most often associated with the 1980s. Such an approach is any unilateral attempt by an acquiring firm to gain control of an acquisition target without the approval of the firm's management or board of directors, that is, a hostile takeover. In many cases, this type of approach followed the "nibbler" strategy in which the acquiring firm bought from just under 5% of the stock of the acquisition target to 25% or more. (It should be noted that any purchase of 5% of the stock of a public company must be accompanied by registration with the SEC indicating the amount of stock purchased and purchaser's intentions with respect to the company.) Typically, when the nibbler strategy was employed, the acquiring firm bought a stake and then made a tender offer for the rest of the stock. Often the acquiring firm was in an ideal position to profit. Either (1) enough stock is purchased without paying a premium to substantially lower the effective cost of the acquisition or (2) the acquiring firm subsequently sells the partial stake at a substantial premium back to the target firm or to a "white knight" bidder.

The completely unnegotiated approach has been used much less frequently in recent years, however, for a number of reasons:

- Some states have enacted laws to guard against such actions.
- Stock market volatility has caused outcomes to be far less predictable.
- It is much more difficult to get financing from banks, insurance companies, and the junk bond market for these transactions.

In the case of commercial bank acquisitions, the opportunistic and completely unnegotiated approaches are rarely used. By far, the friendly persuasion approach is most often observed. Because the industry is so highly regulated, anything other than a negotiated acquisition is generally not feasible.[3]

Using Brokers and Finders

In the early stages of the acquisition process, it may be necessary to employ the services of an intermediary other than an investment banker. This is especially true if the acquiring bank (or a bank seeking to be acquired) is a small- or medium-sized institution. A *broker* studies the bank and its objectives, prepares a description of the desired transaction, helps the bank to determine the best strategy to follow in finding an acquisition target (or an acquiring institution), and assists in negotiating the terms of the transaction. A *finder* serves only to introduce the two institutions. There are varying degrees of services that can be offered between these two extremes.

Typically, neither brokers nor finders are required by state law to be licensed. However, if the transfer of real estate is involved, the rules concerning real estate brokerage may apply. If the transaction involves the sale of stock instead of assets, federal securities laws require that a broker be a registered securities dealer.

The right intermediary can be of great assistance in a number of areas. A broker can analyze the structure of each institution and suggest an appropriate approach to the acquisition target. A broker also can aid in the negotiating process by acting as a buffer to encourage more open discussions than may be possible between the acquiring bank and the acquisition target.

The relationship between the bank and the intermediary will depend on the size of the institution. If the bank is small, there may be a single-transaction arrangement to find a suitable acquisition or a suitable acquiring bank. In either case, the selling institution generally pays the intermediary's fee. If the bank is larger, the acquisition team or the merger-and-acquisition department will have staff with the primary responsibilities of an intermediary. Alternatively, a larger bank may use the services of a broker or finder, keeping the intermediary on a retainer.

The fee of an intermediary is contingent on the completion of the transaction and represents some percentage of the value of the transaction. The fee is most often based on the Lehman formula or the "5–4–3–2–1 formula." That is:

- 5% is paid on the first $1 million of the transaction
- 4% on the amount from $1 million to $2 million
- 3% on the amount from $2 million to $3 million
- 2% on the amount from $3 million to $4 million
- 1% on any amount in excess of $4 million

However, in small transactions, the intermediary's fee can range between 5% and 10% of the amount of the transaction. Also, a fixed percentage, instead of a declining scale, may be used in transactions of all sizes. In the event that the broker has special knowledge and expertise about the banking industry, a premium above the Lehman fee may be assessed. Thus, the fee will depend not only the amount of the transaction, but also on the services rendered and the expertise of the intermediary.

If a broker performs services beyond simply finding an eventual buyer or seller, a purely contingent fee may be inappropriate. This will be particularly true if the intermediary is retained to find an appropriate acquisition target. In this case, the broker may require (1) payment based on time spent in the search and analysis, perhaps with a retainer against which time is charged, and (2) a contingent fee based on the amount of a completed transaction. There may even be incentive clauses in the agreement. Such clauses are most common in the case of a bank seeking to be acquired. A fixed percentage may be paid up to a specified transaction amount with a higher percentage for amounts above the specified level.

The arrangement between the bank and the intermediary should be documented in a written agreement. The specifics of this agreement should include:

- The exact parties in the transaction.
- Whether the intermediary is retained on an exclusive or nonexclusive basis. (The agreement is typically nonexclusive, giving a bank the right to deal with other institutions not introduced through the intermediary.)
- A statement that the broker will assist in negotiations if requested by the contracting bank.
- The definition of a completed transaction. (This can be either all assets, all shares, or some fraction thereof.)

- The fee structure of the arrangement.
- The method in which the proceeds of a completed sale are valued. (For example, securities exchanged will be valued based on prices stipulated in the definitive agreement to complete the transaction.)
- A commitment not to disclose any information identified for nondisclosure by the directors or management of the contracting bank.
- The terms under which the arrangement may be terminated.

The most important element in securing the services of a broker or finder is to find an intermediary whose judgment can be trusted. In this way, the contracting bank can avail itself confidently of services that otherwise may not be available to it.

Defending Against Acquisitions

The issue of unsolicited and unwanted bids for the bank is addressed by methods used to defend against such overtures. In some cases, the buy-out of executives employed by the acquisition target made too expensive through "golden parachutes." In other cases, defenses of many varieties, including "poison pills," are used to discourage unwanted solicitations. In all cases, these measures must be kept in perspective. The goal of directors and management always should be to maximize shareholder wealth, which maximization sometimes is associated with an acquisition. Defenses should not conflict with this objective. The correct balance in this trade-off is sometimes difficult to achieve.

The Use of Golden Parachutes

Golden parachutes are compensation packages that cushion the effect of unemployment for an employee after control of the firm has changed hands. Essentially, the employee is offered special payments for leaving the firm if the employee's job is eliminated as a result of the acquisition. From the perspective of the acquisition target, a golden parachute should help reduce resistance to the acquisition as a result of the employee's concern for self-interests. With fewer concerns about personal security, the employee will negotiate in the best interests of the shareholders, who will, in turn, receive the highest price for their stock.

However, the extensive use of these arrangements during the early 1980s drew criticism from institutional investors and regulators. Huge payouts seem to fly in the face of the objective of financial management—to maximize shareholder wealth. The debate about golden parachutes is part of the debate surrounding executive compensation. The main thesis is that executives should be compensated for creating shareholder wealth. To the extent that golden parachutes reward executives that perform so poorly that their companies require a bailout, the associated compensation cannot be justified. For this reason, golden parachutes have become more associated with defenses against unwanted acquisition overtures.

The actual parachute arrangements can be observed at three different levels:

- The *golden parachute* is offered to top executives.
- The *silver parachute* is designed for middle managers and their peers.

- The *tin parachute* covers lower-level employees.

The payment formulas differ depending on the version of the parachute being employed.

The parachute is activated through triggers. A single-trigger releases the parachute if there is a change in control of the firm. This could involve as little as a 20% purchase of stock by an acquiring firm and, thus, allows the executive to leave with little real provocation. A double-trigger involves, first, a change in control of the firm which begins a probationary period. The second trigger is pulled if the employee is terminated after the probationary period.

The efforts of institutional investors and regulators to eliminate excessive payouts under golden parachutes and other compensation plans culminated in specific provisions of the Deficit Reduction Act of 1984. Any severance package exceeding three times an executive's average compensation for the five years prior to change in control lost its tax deduction for the company and created a 20% excise tax for the departing executive. The permissible multiple was set at 2.99 times the five-year base by the Internal Revenue Service. Amendments to the act in 1989 refined some of the concepts of the original act:

- The composition of the base amount.
- The types of employees that would be considered highly paid and eligible for golden parachutes.
- A one-year period of time that must elapse between the effective date of the golden parachute and the date of change of control.

It should be emphasized that the golden parachute can no longer be used to block an acquisition while it is underway. Also, as all executive compensation comes under closer scrutiny by the SEC, the golden parachute will be subject to increasing disclosure.

Generally speaking, the golden parachute should be considered as part of a total compensation package for an executive, not as simply a mechanism for future defense against acquisition. The compensation committee of the board of directors should evaluate appropriateness, cost/benefit relationships, and acceptability by shareholders when establishing base compensation and the golden parachute.

Other Acquisition Defenses

Poison pills are rights distributed to shareholders that allow them to buy additional shares under certain defined circumstances and can be used to discourage unwanted solicitations. Many are referred to as shareholder rights plans or shareholder protection plans. There is no evidence of the effectiveness of these measures. Indeed, it appears unlikely that even one announced acquisition has been frustrated solely by defensive mechanisms against acquisition. However, it is entirely possible that acquisitions that were still in the conceptual stage have not been pursued because of apparent obstacles to their completion.

Poison pills take a number of forms:

- The "flip-in" right permits shareholders to buy additional stock at a price far above prevailing market levels. However, should the bank be threatened with an unwanted acquisition, the price of additional stock becomes much more attractive. For example, if a tender offer is presented for 30% of the shares, existing shareholders can buy more stock at the rate of two shares for the prevailing market price of one share. (The level of stock ownership by the acquiring firm at which the provision becomes effective is referred to as the kick-in threshold.) The objective is to increase the number of shares outstanding and, presumably, the total cost of the acquisition.

- A "flip-over" pill is a second line of defense. If the acquirer is successful in gaining control, the original shareholders have the right to buy shares of the acquiring firm at prices much lower than the prevailing market price. The objective is to demonstrate the potential dilution of the acquirer's stock.

- A "back-end" pill increases the leverage of the firm when the kick-in threshold is reached. Debt securities are issued to shareholders, thereby increasing the liabilities that must be paid by the acquiring bank.

Poison pills have generally survived the court battles over their legality and are not frequently rescinded when institutional investors challenge them in the context of corporate governance.

While poison pills are essentially shareholder provisions, *poison securities* are issued with provisions that accomplish similar outcomes.

- "Poison shares" have normal voting rights in most circumstances but receive much more voting power in the event of an unwanted solicitation or attack. For example, preferred shares may be nonvoting or have one vote per share. When the bank is attacked, each preferred shareholder may have 10 votes.
- "Poison puts" are attached to debt securities—bonds, notes, and other debt instruments. When an attack is launched or control changes hands, the debt securities become immediately callable and must be redeemed.

Financial engineering may also be used to ward off unwanted bids for the bank:

- A "self-tender" is the large scale repurchase of shares in response to unsolicited bids. This channels cash to shareholders who accept the offers, generally priced above market price, and reduces the number of shares outstanding, usually pushing up the stock price. If borrowed funds are used to purchase the shares, this approach also increases the leverage of the bank. Of course, such a strategy will be impacted by capital level considerations.
- An "in-house ESOP" or employee stock ownership plan can hold a substantial percentage of the bank's outstanding stock. The premise of this approach is that the employees of the bank will vote against a hostile bid to buy the bank.
- "Pension parachutes" are designed to discourage unsolicited bids that are at least partially

motivated by overfunded pension plans. During the 1980s, many acquisition targets were attractive because overfunded pension plans could be terminated and the surplus funding captured, as long as employees in the plan were given an adequate substitute for the terminated plan. The pension parachute removed the economic incentive for this tactic. One type of provision prevents the acquiring firm from gaining access to the pension fund. Another immediately increases benefits to retired and existing employees if control of the firm changes hands.

All of these defenses should be considered by any bank that has a strong inclination to remain independent. They may, in fact, be appropriate for a closely held bank with shareholders closely involved in the bank's management. However, if the ownership is widely held and, particularly, if shareholders include institutional investors, management should be wary of instituting policies that can be interpreted as preventing transactions that would enhance shareholder wealth.

Managing the Transition

Perhaps even more than with a merger, an acquisition can lead to potentially devastating impacts on productivity of the acquired institution and, accordingly, shareholder value. However, the basics of managing the transition are similar with respect to communications and consolidation of the two institution.[4] Special effort should be exerted to guard against the disintegration of morale within the acquired institution:

- Communicate the impending change as soon as negotiations will permit.
- Share the strategic plan with the employees of the acquired institution as soon as possible.
- Be prepared to be flexible and creative with necessary job changes, softening the adverse effects for employees as much as possible.
- Invest in the development and retraining of those employees who remain.

The communications process should include meetings with employees, factual press releases, accurate communication with the banking community served. This may be more difficult for the management of the acquired institution to accomplish than in the case of a merger. Top management, when faced with an acquisition, may tend to withdraw from the public forum and confer behind closed doors with investment bankers and attorneys, leaving rumors to develop and spread unchecked. Communication to employees who will lose their positions should be accomplished as quickly as possible, with an explanation of why their jobs have been eliminated. Generous severance packages can help soften this blow. For those who remain, special performance bonuses for help during the transition period can provide morale boosting incentives.

The strategic plan of the acquiring bank will reduce uncertainty by providing a philosophical road map as to the direction of the institution. Major changes undertaken by management will appear less capricious, easing the transition. Also, if employees understand the direction of the bank, they can contribute more to implementation. For example, if staff employees understand the overall objectives and are asked to give specific suggestions about improving workflow or procedures, their reactions will be more responsive and productivity is likely to increase.

The necessary job reductions should be approached with as much compassion as possible. One way of doing this is to make office services available to displaced workers. An outplacement officer can also be appointed to assist in the preparation of resumes, mailings, contacts with other companies, and other helpful services. Sometimes the use of early retirement offers can reduce the need for across-the-board job cuts. The most successful early retirement programs offer smaller actuarial reduction in retirement benefits, additional age or service credits, and other non-pension benefits such as one-time payments or post-retirement health care benefits. If the acquired bank has a stock option plan and the value of the stock of the acquired bank increased as a result of the takeover, some of the key executives may be in a favorable position for early retirement. From the perspective of the acquiring bank, the expense of inducements in the early retirement offer is lowered by these stock market dynamics. It is sound business practice to treat displaced executives fairly. If they are angry about the treatment that they received, they may cause problems during the transition, either while operating from their homes or after they have relocated in a competing institution.

Investing in the development and retraining of employees is especially critical in management ranks. This is true despite an organizational focus on downsizing. The need is clearly driven by changing corporate strategies, culture clashes, and organizational uncertainties. One way to approach this is to help managers move out of their "functional" mindsets and into a more organizational perspective. For example, managers from all functional areas can meet with the president of the bank one day per week, with questions that have arisen during the week through interaction with their staff. These questions should range from the procedural to the philosophical. If the sessions are structured in such a way that the president responds to varied questions from the managers and discussion among the managers is encouraged, the managers will learn more about the entire organization and the mindset of senior management. Uncertainties are resolved and managers can perform more effectively as a team.

Taking these extra steps when a bank is acquired by another institution will help smooth the transition. They will help ensure that a single, integrated and focused culture can emerge and that trust and loyalty are preserved.

Using Acquisitions to Diversify

Acquisitions can be a powerful tool in diversifying both geographic presence and product mix. Two examples of the use of acquisition strategy help illustrate—National Australia Bank and KeyCorp.

National Australia Bank and Michigan National

In February 1995, National Australia Bank, Ltd. agreed to acquire Michigan National Corp. for $1.56 billion. The almost $9 billion Michigan National had been identified as a takeover target for some time because of inconsistent financial performance. In fact, institutional investors held large stakes in Michigan National and had pushed for a sale of the bank. The size of the acquisition target makes this combination one of the largest takeovers of a U.S. bank by a foreign financial institution.

National Australia began acquiring regional banks in 1987, with a strategy of identifying institutions that would benefit from its strong balance sheet and efficient cost structure. Its subsidiaries in the United Kingdom include Yorkshire Bank PLC, Clydesdale Bank PLC, and Northern Bank Ltd. In Ireland, National Australia owns National Irish Bank Ltd. and is negotiating the purchase of Trustee Savings Bank. In 1992, it also purchased Bank of New Zealand Ltd.

The Australian bank had apparently been pursuing Michigan National for some time, its attraction being the strong deposit base which reduces its reliance on the wholesale money market. The acquiring bank had observed Michigan National since 1989 and the first discussions took place in 1992. This is the Australian institution's first entry into the U.S. market and it appears that its location in a blue-collar manufacturing region was an important factor. (The bank also targeted industrial regions in the United Kingdom.) The acquiring institution offered a substantial premium for the acquisition—$110 per share in cash when the stock was trading in the low-90s range. National Australia plans to increase earnings by cutting costs and to use Michigan National, with its 191 branches and 4,000 staff, as a springboard into the rest of the United States.

KeyCorp and AutoFinance Group

In March 1995, KeyCorp of New York and AutoFinance Group, Inc. of Chicago announced a definitive agreement for KeyCorp to acquire AutoFinance (AFG). Unlike the National Australia offer, the KeyCorp bid is a stock swap. Under the terms of the agreement, AFG common shareholders will receive KeyCorp common stock valued at $16.50 per share for each share of AFG stock. A collar of between .5 and .6 shares of KeyCorp for every one share of AFG has also been established.

AFG is one of the nation's largest finance companies and focuses primarily on loans to non-prime buyers of new and late model used cars. The finance company has developed sophisticated credit evaluation systems and rigorous loan monitoring capabilities. Its affiliation with KeyCorp will give it access to an expanded customer base that it otherwise would not have been able to tap.

From KeyCorp's perspective, AFG helps fulfill one of the bank's primary objectives—to gain a prominent position in national consumer finance. With this acquisition, KeyCorp becomes one of the nation's largest non-captive auto finance companies. AFG complements the bank's operations in other specialty consumer finance business such as marine and recreational vehicle financing, home equity loans, and educational lending. The acquisition effectively expands KeyCorp's $67 billion operation from its present scope of 14 states to the 28 states in which AFG has offices.

The Art of the Deal

As these two contrasting examples illustrate, the art of the acquisition deal is for the acquiring bank to formulate its strategic plan and then use its imagination and resourcefulness to identify the right target to accomplish specific aspects of that plan.

Selected References

Allen, Paul H. "Making Consolidation Work," *The Bankers Magazine*, July/August 1994, pp. 32–37.

Bird, Anat and Richard Israel. "Managing the Acquisition Process," *Strategic Planning*, May/June 1994, pp. 4–9.

Fitch, Thomas. *Dictionary of Banking Terms*, Hauppauge, New York: Barron's Educational Series, Inc., 1990.

Gutknecht, John E. "Mergers, Acquisitions, and Takeovers: Maintaining Morale of Survivors and Protecting Employee," *Academy of Management Executive*, vol. 7, no.3 (1993), pp.26–36.

Rock, Milton L., Robert H. Rock, Martin Sikora. *The Mergers and Acquisitions Handbook*, 2e, New York: McGraw-Hill, 1994.

Endnotes

1 See Chapter 1 for a description of regional agreements that permit bank acquisition across state lines.

2 The Glass-Steagall Act was passed in 1933 and required the separation of commercial banking and investment banking. As part of the Banking Act of 1933, the designation of Glass-Steagall Act is most often associated with four specific sections of the Banking Act—sections 16, 20, 21, and 32. Section 16 prohibits Federal Reserve member banks from purchasing equity securities and from underwriting and dealing in any securities, with the exceptions of (1) U.S. Treasury and federal agency securities and (2) general obligations of states and political subdivisions. Section 20 prohibits member banks from affiliating with firms that are principally engaged in underwriting corporate stocks and bonds. Section 21 makes it a crime for securities underwriters or other securities firms to accept deposits. Section 32 prohibits interlocking directorates between banks and securities firms. Beginning in the late 1980s, Federal Reserve interpretation of these sections has permitted limited activity by commercial banks in securities activities.

3 See Chapter 1 for a description of the regulatory approval process associated with bank mergers and acquisitions.

4 See Chapter 2.

4

Strategic Alliances to Reengineer the Bank

Introduction

As demonstrated in Chapters 2 and 3, the motivation for merging with another institution and making an acquisition can be to expand market share in the current geographic area of operation, to enter new areas, to offer new products, to operate more efficiently, or some combination of these. However, it is not always necessary or desirable to take an equity position in another firm to accomplish these objectives. If the advantage of working with another firm appears to be an advantage that may diminish with time, a *strategic alliance* is more appropriate. Such arrangements can be particularly useful when a bank seeks efficiency improvements and new product offerings.

Reengineering the Bank

In his book *Reengineering the Bank*, Paul Allen provides many useful insights into ways to make a commercial bank more efficient and more profitable. His list of "Jump Start Ideas" for management includes 11 suggestions under two general themes:[1]

Retail Branch Network

1. Reorganize Branch Structure to "Hub-and-Spoke" Configuration (that is, provide customers the services they want in the most convenient location).
2. Close unprofitable branches.
3. Centralize transaction processing.
4. Increase branch automation.
5. Streamline transaction processing procedures (including the evaluation of ATM outsourcing).
6. Tailor products and services.
7. Streamline administrative functions.

Consumer Liability Products

8. Change existing product lines (including the introduction of new products requiring little or no additional cost to deliver).
9. Charge for tailored service/higher cost transactions.
10. Explore new or increased pricing opportunities.
11. Eliminate "escape clauses" and waivers from all liability product lines.

Interestingly, at least five of these 11 suggestions can be at least partially accomplished through strategic alliances:

- Centralize transaction processing.
- Increase branch automation.
- Streamline transactions processing procedures.
- Tailor products and services.
- Introduce new products requiring little or no additional cost to deliver.

The wisdom of addressing these issues is readily apparent. The bank's customers are continually exploring ways to become more efficient in their own operations. For example, in the 1980s, large U.S. companies had an average of 20 bank relationships. By 1993, this average had fallen to 15.4. It appears that corporate treasurers are attempting to reduce the time spent evaluating and tracking bank services. A survey by Ernst & Young in 1994 shows, on average, that two banks account for 59% of a corporation's fees for banking services.[2]

Shell Oil presents a good example of how corporations are attempting to streamline their cash management operations. Shell operates a complex cash management system partially because it has its own credit card service, generating $5 billion in annual inflows and outflows. Despite the fact that the company had gone through a consolidation in 1990 that resulted in the centralization of transaction processing in Houston, Texas, Shell undertook a benchmarking exercise with five corporations in other industries. Finding that the other corporations used much simpler cash management operations, Shell began to reengineer the process. Of the 600 bank accounts that the firm maintained, some could no longer be cost-justified. The reengineering team set about to reduce the number of accounts, combine as many services as possible, and reduce the number of data transmissions and overdrafts. The result of this exercise was the elimination of non-value added work and a cost reduction to 30% to 35% from 1990 to 1993.

To meet the challenge of such a trend, commercial banks are increasingly forming strategic alliances, particularly with technology firms to provide more efficient service for both corporate and retail clients.

Successful strategic alliances will benefit both the bank and the technology partner. The results will be to:

- Increase skills and core competencies.
- Share the costs and risks.
- Fundamentally change the way the bank thinks about and uses technology.

The costs for the bank will include the out-of-pocket expense associated with developing and implementing the new technology and a significant time commitment on the part of senior management to bring together the human resources and talents of the two entities.

Centralizing Transactions Processing

A number of banks have instituted programs that use the concept of strategic alliance to improve efficiency.

Banc One

In a recent interview for *The American Banker*, John B. McCoy, CEO of Banc One Corporation, made the following comments:

> A remarkable change has happened in our business. For a long time, the small bank had better returns than the larger ones. That has changed. In our company, the most profitable banks are over $1 billion. We asked ourselves, why aren't the smaller banks as successful as they used to be? . . . Competition and product line are more sophisticated than ever before. For example, at any one time, our mortgage company has over 30 products to offer.

Because of these cost and profit dynamics, Banc One has undertaken a hybrid approach to the question of centralization vs. decentralization. For some time, the focus of management has been to be a super community bank—to offer banking services to individuals and small- and medium-sized businesses in its 81 banks. At the same time, Banc One management has recognized that it is not cost effective to operate 81 different securities companies or mortgage banks.

The organization plans to achieve economies of scale by initiating new software applications that will help it solve the problem of incompatible systems in its far-flung network of acquired banks. The banking institution will consolidate 81 separate bank charters into 13—one for each state in which it has operations. This new initiative is part of Banc One's ultimate objective of becoming a truly national bank. The integration of these systems will involve a common platform and common systems, allowing the bank to realize significant economies of scale. The new technology-supported plan is estimated to have saved Banc One $125 million in 1994 and is projected to save as much as $200 million in 1995.

In connection with this overall efficiency-enhancing effort, Banc One has entered into a strategic alliance with Electronic Data Systems (EDS) to build Strategic Banking System. The goals of this ambitious arrangement are:

- To replace 15 major transaction processing systems.
- To tie into 50 additional banking systems.
- To integrate total customer and market information for cross-selling purposes.
- To make the system available to the bank's 883 branches.

Norwest has joined the strategic alliance as one of the additional banking systems and has fully operationalized the customer-and-market-information module. It should also be noted that because of the wide scope of the project, there have been delays in operationalizing the deposit and credit systems. Nevertheless, this is an example of the kind of economies of scale that are being pursued in the banking industry.

First Tennessee Bank

Centralizing the transactions process with the help of First Tennessee Bank offers another attractive strategic alliance. First Tennessee is headquartered in Memphis, also the headquarters of Federal Express Corporation, the overnight delivery company. Federal Express packages are shipped to Memphis, where they are sorted and then shipped to their final destinations. First Express, the service offered by First Tennessee Bank, operates on the same principle. Each night, banks send their checks to Memphis via Federal Express or other overnight courier. The checks are processed at the Federal Express hub within three hours—run through reader/sorters and sorted by city and bank. By 8 a.m., all checks have been shipped to the cities of the banks on which they have been drawn.

First Tennessee plays an important role because small banks do not have the resources to develop a high-speed and highly efficient clearing facility. It is estimated that as many as 10,000 banks are still processing their own checks. Further advances in alternative means of check presentment will likely lead to a decline in the number of paper checks being handled and a corresponding over capacity in check processing departments of many banks. In turn, a centralized, third-party check clearing system can offer important efficiencies.

Multinet International Bank

The centralization of transactions processing can also be enhanced with strategic alliances in the area of foreign currencies. In August 1994, eight U.S. and Canadian banks formed Multinet International Bank, a new clearinghouse for foreign exchange transactions to be fully operational some time in 1995. The eight founding members of the clearinghouse are Chase Manhattan Bank, First National Bank of Chicago, Royal Bank of Canada, Canadian Imperial Bank of Commerce, Bank of Nova Scotia, Bank of Montreal, National Bank of Canada, and Toronto Dominion Bank.

The combination of the members' individual clearing functions is intended to save time and money by eliminating the need to clear each trade individually. Instead, trades will be netted and only one payment per day per currency will be necessary. The seven currencies that will be traded initially are the U.S. dollar, Canadian dollar, German deutsche mark, Japanese yen, British pound, French franc, and Swiss franc. Both spot transactions and forward contracts will be settled. Once Multinet is fully operational, other banks will also be able to join the network.

TCAM Systems, Inc.

Banks also can achieve efficiencies in the area of securities through new service bureau entrants into the market. A vendor of trading systems for over 15 years, TCAM Systems, Inc. (TCAM) is a notable example. In the early 1980s, TCAM formed a strategic alliance with Dean Witter and became the first technology firm to automatically execute OTC orders in the NASDAQ stock market.[3] Since that time, the firm has introduced a number of innovations in the automation of securities trading.

In mid-1994, TCAM began offering a service bureau. The motivation for this product is that TCAM can reach firms that could not otherwise afford its services. This service bureau offers:

- TCAM's Continuous Trading Processing System, with its order-routing and order-management functions
- TCAM's Traders Aid System for listed, OTC, and international equities trading
- An interface with back-office and settlement systems

The key point is that TCAM has assembled a package of services that can act as a main hub in directing users' trading traffic to the appropriate address.

The communications network of the service bureau includes the following on-line features:

- Automatic execution of trades
- Order routing and order management
- Statements of trading position and profit and loss
- Information from major and regional securities exchanges
- Information from listed and OTC market makers
- Institutional investors buying activity

Examples of other companies that offer variations of these services for financial institutions are ADP, Fidelity, Bear Stearns & Co., and Merrill Lynch. By forming a strategic alliance with one of these firms, a bank can achieve efficiencies in the area of brokerage operations.

Increasing Branch Automation

Branch automation is a concept that sometimes falls short of expectations in the implementation phase. This occurs because whatever inefficiencies existing before branch automation is introduced will continue to exist after it is in place. Thus, the successful implementation of branch automation must take place in the context of strategic goals of management. Once the goals have been identified, then the form of automation that will best support the accomplishment of these goals can be identified and adopted. Important considerations are:

- Reallocation of resources
- Restructuring operating units
- Changing the bank's culture with respect to tasks and work flow

Two examples from outside the banking industry will help illustrate the need to identify *first* the substance of needed change and *then* the form of the change. Both Federal Express and United Parcel Service determined that there was a need for faster information delivery. The development of faxes and computer modems presented a way to satisfy this need. As a result, these forms of communication became an integral part of the work flow of the two firms. Scanning technology was added in the area of package handling and new services that permitted customer feedback through technology were introduced.

Within the financial services field, Countrywide Home Mortgage Loan Corporation identified a need to help its loan officers gain a competitive advantage. Countrywide equipped its loan representatives with portable laptop computers so that they could go to any borrower at any time and any place.

To increase the level of branch automation within the bank, there are five stages that should be followed after the strategies for the institution have been appropriately mapped out:

- Defining technology applications that will fill the bank's information needs
- Evaluating and selecting potential vendors/strategic partners
- Analyzing and justifying cost

- Negotiating viable contracts
- Managing implementation

Defining the appropriate technology applications involves aligning the bank's technology requirements with its overall strategic business plans. System configurations will influence the costs and benefits of any branch automation project. The two basic system configurations are:

- Personal computer-based
- Controller-based

Personal computer-based systems connect intelligent workstations or local area networks (LANs) to host computers that process applications such as demand deposit accounts, savings accounts, time deposit accounts, mortgages, commercial loans, and automobile loans. Since the workstations or LANs are capable of operating without the host, most functions can continue when the host computer is down. *Controller-based systems* connect terminals to mini-computers, or controllers, that are, in turn, linked to the host computer. In some cases, the controllers may be able to work when the host is down. Generally, however, if the host computer fails, the system is rendered inoperable.

It should be noted that the personal computer-based (PC-based) system offers greater flexibility of operation than a comparable controller-based system. Furthermore, through the PC-based configuration, communication among users of the systems is facilitated. A bank that has adopted a product cross-selling philosophy will be better served with the PC-based configuration. A LAN can help a community bank realize large savings in operating efficiency because the LAN is commonly used for data transmission among those authorized to use the network, thus eliminating the need to move paper files in many cases. For a bank that has a large number of branches that should be linked via PC, the appropriate architecture is the wide area network (WAN).

The first step in *evaluating and selecting potential vendors/strategic partners* is preparation of the request for proposal package (RFP). This document will specify the current information systems and the requirements of the branch automation project. The requirements that should be spelled out explicitly are: functional requirements (functions that should be accomplished by the software), technical requirements (specific system constraints to which the branch automation system must conform), performance requirements (minimum objectives for variables such as response time and down time), vendor services requirements (types of professional and support services that will be offered by the vendor), and contractual requirements (those conditions that the bank wants included in any agreement with the vendor). In this way, the bank will be able to identify the right strategic partner to achieve the desired results.

Analyzing and justifying cost will involve first evaluating the work flow. The right strategic partner should exhibit a willingness to assist the bank with this phase of the process. The appropriate work flow assessment will evaluate the costs of current practices, alternative approaches to work flow, synergies that could be captured (that currently are not being realized), and the costs of implementing the optimal system.

Negotiating viable contracts probably will begin even before the strategic partner is selected. Throughout the discussions with potential vendors, the bank should perform on-going SWOT analyses (strengths, weaknesses, opportunities, and threats). The actual contract with the selected vendors should also specify the critical elements of the relationship in all areas, leaving nothing to be assumed (or misunderstood).

Managing implementation is the last phase of the process. Unless the bank and its strategic partner are committed to this part of the project, the earlier phases will have little impact. Managers, vendors, and system users should be actively involved in new systems implementation. The essential elements of managing implementation are:

- Quality assurance
- Integration of business operations with the new system
- System architecture management
- Managing expectations of participants during the implementation phase

With the right strategic partner in the process of branch automation, a bank can increase its employees' productivity and efficiency, while offering better service to its customers.

Streamlining Transactions Processing Procedures

One of the most important ways in which transactions processing can be accomplished is through modifying the payments system and using automated teller machines more effectively. In many cases, these can be accomplished through strategic alliances with technology firms and/or other commercial banks.

Electronic Check Presentment

Through *electronic check presentment* (ECP), information on a check may be shared electronically much faster than the physical check can be cleared. In a sense, regulators are forcing banks to improve the efficiency with which the payments mechanism is managed. Regulation CC (of the Federal Reserve System) requires banks to make funds available within certain maximum time periods after checks have been deposited. If the payee and payor banks are in the same Federal Reserve check-processing zone, the maximum hold for the check is one business day. If the two institutions are not in the same check-processing zone, the maximum hold is four business days. Notwithstanding the time limits imposed by Reg CC, it can require six to ten days for an out-of-town check to go through the system and for the advice to be returned to the payee bank. Clearly, the problem is that if such a check is drawn on an account with insufficient funds, the payee bank could have already released the funds to its customer. This situation naturally encourages the development of more efficient clearing systems.

With ECP, the payee bank (bank in which the check has been deposited) scans the magnetic ink character recognition (MICR) line. This information is wired to the payor bank (bank upon which the check has been written). If there are insufficient funds for the check, the check is flagged overnight instead of several days, or even a week, later.

ECP standards and practices are being developed through the Electronic Check Clearing House Organization (ECCHO), with member banks including:

- Citicorp
- Bank of America
- Chase Manhattan
- Chemical Bank
- NationsBank

A total of more than 60 banks are members of ECCHO. The ECP procedure is being tested in Michigan and California. It is estimated that as many as 1,000 banks currently have the computer capacity to receive some sort of electronic check information.

While there are obvious benefits, the cost of ECP is also substantial. A bank that would like to send checks electronically must invest $50,000 plus training costs. An institution that plans to receive checks electronically should expect to spend $200,000 to $300,000. However, the availability of such timely information can be turned into a fee-generating operation. For example, a corporate bank customer that has deposited a check for goods can be advised if the check will not be honored before the merchandise is shipped. Also, ECP can eliminate many of the delays associated with check processing for small, remote banks that have correspondent relationships with large banks. The cost of the system can be partially offset by fees from providing advance clearing information.

Ultimately, however, ECP represents significant savings for banks. There is reduced dependence on processing equipment and transportation services, float savings, and earlier return check notification. Under the conventional system, each time a check is inserted into a sorter, there is a new opportunity for it to be mishandled or for it to jam the sorting equipment. Also, because the most critical information on the check—account number and payment amounts—is sent electronically, there is no need to ship the physical document in the most expedient (and expensive) manner. ECP links the payee bank with the payor bank overnight, thereby exceeding the Reg CC requirements. If necessary, the payor bank can advise the payee bank of a no-pay decision even before the paper checks are shipped by the payee bank, providing the payee bank ample opportunity to withhold funds from the depositor of the check.

The Federal Reserve System is also examining the ECP technology. With a pilot program of several banks, the Federal Reserve is initiating the sending and receiving of ECP information by participating banks.

Through these strategic alliances with either the private sector or the regulatory sector, banks are attempting to achieve efficiencies that could not otherwise be realized.

Imaging Technology

The Federal Reserve has long been a champion of further efficiencies in the payments sytem, with *truncating*, the ultimate efficiency in check processing, being the ultimate goal. Truncating is the process in which cancelled checks are held by the customer's bank, or by another bank in the collection system, and not returned to the check writer in the account statement. Checks can either be truncated at the bank of first deposit or by a Federal Reserve bank.

Although almost 12 million checks are truncated by Federal Reserve banks each month, the greatest interest appears to be from the U.S. Treasury Department and small financial institutions. Most bankers seem unwilling to forgo receipt of the physical checks. Electronic check presentment (ECP), alone, does not appear to be acceptable to the vast majority of bankers. On the other hand, imaging technology can increase the appeal of less paper-dependent payment mechanisms.

Employing *imaging technology* in check clearing means that a bank would receive graphical images of the checks drawn against it instead of the actual paper check. The Federal Reserve apparently has much interest in this technology because it can provide backup support for truncating. Using images can assist the payor bank in such areas as pay-or-no-pay decisions and signature verifications. Such systems are being developed by IBM, Unisys, NCR, and Banctec Systems.

The biggest technical challenge in imaging the check clearing process is the correct interpretation of the written check amounts. Character amount recognition or character amount read (CAR) means that personnel need not manually read the numerals written in the courtesy amount boxes of checks. The challenge is that there are as many as 30 different ways that checks are written. The problems with CAR tend to center around three factors:

- The condition or readability of the physical checks
- The various ways that customers write checks

- The variety of locations for the courtesy amount box on the checks

Huntington Bancshares (Columbus, Ohio) has formed a strategic alliance with Unisys to deploy imaging technology. Within the first 4 months of operation, the percentage of checks read correctly by the system increased from 35% to 44%. By 1997, the Huntington hopes to have this percentage up to 50%. This potentially could imply as much as a 50% reduction in the personnel cost associated with check clearing. Huntington is increasing the effectiveness of the technology by redesigning deposit and loan payment tickets, including special shaded boxes, dollar signs, and other features, to improve CAR.

KeyCorp (Albany, New York) has formed a strategic alliance with BankAmerica and IBM. Once again, the long-term objective is to read 50% of the checks. The IBM system uses neural network technology to locate and interpret the courtesy amount box on corporate checks and other items. This type of technology uses DIDMs (document identification and description modules, pronounced "diddoms") to help locate the payment amount and interpret the amounts based on past interpretations of similar-looking numbers.

National City (Cleveland, Ohio) selected NCR for its strategic partner in streamlining the transactions. While the bank plans to be able to read 50% of the checks it processes, it is possible that the read rate could go as high as 60%. National City's objective is, of course, to significantly reduce unit costs.

Entering a strategic alliance with a technology firm to institute imaging technology is a long-term commitment—at least five years. During this period, it probably will be necessary to:

- Upgrade the bank's systems and telecommunications infrastructure.
- Reengineer bank operations and processes.
- Retrain bank employees.
- Redesign certain bank products.

This implies major efforts in the areas of internal and external marketing concerning the benefits of the new technology.

Furthermore, while the maximum cost associated with ECP is $200,000 to $300,000, installing imaging capability—hardware and software—can require millions of dollars. Also, in many cases, the strategic partners in the venture generally cannot provide completely accurate cost estimates because there is not yet sufficient experience with imaging applications. It should be noted that a large-scale operation is necessary to justify the costs. If there are relatively few employees in the area to be enhanced with imaging technology, the investment cannot be justified on the basis of cost alone. However, it may be justifiable from the standpoint of using the same number of people to do more work, that is, increasing productivity.

Signet Bank

Signet Bank was one of the first banks to completely convert the proof of deposit (POD) function to imaging technology.[4] POD has long been a manual process since it requires the comparison of handwritten amounts on checks and deposit slips. Using imaging technology in this function is an important step in improving bank productivity.

Imaging technology also significantly improves the work environment in the check processing area. Typically, in this fast-paced operational area, two people who want to converse must shout to hear each other. Now at Signet Bank, the same people may whisper and still hear each other while the speed of processing has dramatically increased over conventional systems. An average, conventional check-clearing operation can clear about 1,400 checks per hour. The Signet system clears more than 20,000 per hour. The imaging technlogy has reduced the number of checks that must be processed manually by 42%, enabling personnel to balance and settle more quickly and to more easily meet nightly deadlines.

The cost of the system for Signet Bank is approximately $7.5 million. However, a large check-clearing operation can require as much as $10 million per year in personnel costs for the encoding staff alone. A 40% to 50% reduction in manual encoding can create significant savings. Signet Bank has projected that it will recover its initial investment in less than five years.

Signet hopes to expand the use of imaging technology to offer services to its commercial customers that will help it retain and better serve these clients. Future plans include exporting images to account reconciliation systems, that is, expediting the statement generation and delivery process. The bank also plans to use imaging technology to transfer lockbox images directly to the accounts payable systems of corporate clients. Such services will enable Signet Bank to differentiate itself in the market place of commercial banking.

Interbank Strategic Alliances and the ATM

A major trend is developing that involves banks forming strategic alliances to develop new streams of fee income while sharing operational expense. The first such alliance occurred in 1992 when Banc One, Corestates Financial, PNC Financial, and Society Corporation formed a joint venture called Electronic Payment Services (EPS). The new company represented an important step in the development of a truly national ATM system. Such a system ultimately will lower transactions costs for customers while increasing fee income for banks because there will be no non-financial middleman.

This first alliance has been followed by other movements in the industry in this direction. Many banks and regional networks have now entered into discussions of collaborations. Some of these discussions have resulted in alliances of ATM systems. The Yankee 24 Network in New England has merged with the NYCE Automated Teller Machine Network in New York. Cash Station in Illinois has merged with Magic Line in Michigan.

These alliances and others like them will enable bank participants to offer services in a more streamlined technological environment, to share the cost of developing and operating a commodity service needed by the participants, to share fee income being generated by a growing population of ATM users, and to generate income outsourcing the service to other financial institutions.

Tailoring Products and Services

If there is one over-arching theme in the transformation of the commercial banking industry, it is that bankers should not consider themselves merely managers of securities, loans, deposits, and premises. Instead, bankers are increasingly managers of information. From this perspective, the future products and services offered by banks will be driven by this redefinition of commercial banking.

Successful reengineering cannot be accomplished simply by cutting costs. In tailoring products and services that will compete successfully with those offered by nonbank financial services firms, a bank should develop a strong ability to assess its costs and its clients. To do this effectively, effective *management information systems (MIS)* are essential. Examples of basic questions that good MIS will address are:

- What is the cost of offering a traditional checking account? (Necessary to accurately price checking account services.)
- How many customers actually come into a branch to conduct banking business? (Necessary to value the branch appropriately.)
- What is the value of the relationship with a particular customer? (Necessary to decide what resources to devote to that client.)

The trend in banking is to organize information around product line revenues so that a reasonable allocation of capital to these product lines can be made. Gathering data and creating information that will facilitate this process helps bank managers make better business decisions. In many cases, information and product line management can be best accomplished through strategic alliances with technology firms.

PNC Bank and Hogan Systems

PNC Bank of Pittsburgh and Hogan Systems of Dallas worked together to create the Earnings Analysis System (EAS) to manage information on a bank-wide basis. PNC helped Hogan to develop the system and tested it in the pilot stage. PNC provided the management, accounting, and banking expertise, while Hogan provided expertise in technology and database management.

When PNC decided to change from a generally autonomous method of management for each of its acquired banks, a line-of-business structure approach was adopted. This necessitated the development of a system that would cut across the traditional legal-entity lines that separated member banks in the PNC organization. EAS permits PNC to extract information at the customer level for every transaction. Profitability can be viewed in several different dimensions—along organizational, product, or customer lines. For example, it is possible to analyze revenues and expenses for all autombile loans in all banks in the PNC system.

Hogan's EAS is now available to other commercial banks. The approximate cost ranges from $350,000 to $2 million. The advisability of such an investment can only be determined by examining the size of the asset portfolio and operating expense budget that such a system would help to manage. Nevertheless, it is clear that appropriate decisions about products and services can only be made when both revenues and costs are well understood.

Liberty Bancorp, Systematics, and Hewlett Packard

At the end of the 1980s, Liberty Bancorp of Oklahoma City had survived the difficult oil-industry recession in the Southwest. The institution had emerged from recapitalization as one of only a few banks in Texas and Oklahoma with assets in excess of $1 billion that had not required government assistance. However, the bank's managers realized that the information systems of Liberty were inadequate and presented a serious problem. There was no overall strategy for information management. Each department had created its own database, while similar information was available through the central host system. This produced a duplication of effort and raised questions about the consistency of the information. From the customer's perspective, conducting business with Liberty was like conducting business with several, distinctly different smaller banks. There were even four different phone systems—a holdover from acquisitions during the 1980s.

In 1991, Liberty initiated a five-year plan that assumed up-to-date information systems. To support this plan, Liberty needed to reevaluate completely its information and telephone systems. The bank elected to move to a client/server architecture with open systems technology. The open system technology made it possible to incorporate the existing systems. The client/server architecture permitted departments of the bank to share information that had been collected and managed centrally. The server (central unit) represented a central information storehouse while individual departments tapped into the information as needed. Universal email, spreadsheets, and word processing programs tied the whole system together. This system would create a more efficient bank operation and provide better service for bank clients.

However, the system could not be realized without a strategic alliance. Liberty had a long-standing relationship with its facilities manager, Systematics Financial Services. Liberty brought to the alliance its plan for systems integration. Systematics brought to the alliance bank application software experience in a centralized computer environment. However, neither had client/server and open architecture expertise. Thus, a third member of the strategic alliance was needed. Hewlett-Packard (HP) was selected a leader in client/server and related techologies. Liberty also insisted that Systematics and HP form a strategic alliance to redevelop the bank's systems so that the project represented a strong 3-way commitment by the firms involved.

Each of these companies gains considerable advantage in this arrangement. Systematics has gained expertise in the design of bank software systems that represents the greatest growth potential for the future—that is, client/server architecture. HP has gained considerable experience in banking industry applications. Liberty Bancorp has gained in a number of ways:

- Reengineering the workflow will allow the bank to grow without increasing the work force. A 15% productivity gain will be realized by eliminating redundant data entry.
- More effective customer service will be possible. Tellers will be able to sell products and

services. Platform officers will be able to offer financial services instead of simply opening new accounts.

- In light of these advantages, the cost of the new systems is not prohibitive—the equivalent of the cost of five years of the previous systems. The cost reductions that will be realized after this initial investment will ultimately make Liberty Bancorp much more efficient and arguably an industry leader in customer service.

Introducing New Products and Services

Strategic alliances can also be used to offer bank clients new products and services that can represent little or no additional cost to deliver. There are increasingly more examples of how this can be accomplished in payment mechanisms and investment alternatives.

MasterBanking

MasterBanking has been introduced by MasterCard to offer home banking and electronic bill payment. A strategic alliance between MasterCard and Independent Bankers Association of America (IBAA) makes it possible for smaller banks to provide these services to their customers and earn fee income in the process.

MasterBanking is a nationwide service that permits depositors to make payments at any time and from any location. The system will support personal computers, screen phones, or telephones. Customers give instructions via one of these media and receive a confirmation number when the transaction is complete. Should the customer have any questions about the transaction, he or she may telephone to confirm the details. Other services include intrabank transfers, balance inquiries, and paid and cleared items. In the future, MasterBanking will provide access to investment brokerage, yellow pages, and news retrieval services.

Since this service permits such flexibility with respect to transactions and location, it is more appropriately referred to as interactive financial services, rather than home banking. Several years ago, the concept of home banking was enthusiastically introduced but received little acceptance by retail banking customers. However, the environment for remote banking has changed considerably since that time. Consumers want to bank when it is most convenient for them because of increasing time pressures. Moreover, technology is now more widely accepted and easier to use. Now, offering remote capabilities can be an important component of bank services.

Recognizing these trends, IBAA Bancard has formed a strategic alliance with MasterCard to make it easy for IBAA members (primarily smaller, community banks) to participate in MasterBanking. IBAA members are provided a cost-effective, turnkey operation that includes customer service and marketing. Furthermore, the products carry the name of the IBAA member bank so that this arrangement is effectively a private-label package of remote financial services.

Fees that the IBAA member charges to its customers are determined by that member bank. These fees are clearly an attractive aspect of MasterBanking. In addition, bank customers will have an increased tendency to consolidate their banking activities with one institution that provides such comprehensive services. This strategic alliance means that smaller institutions can be a part of the development of the "information superhighway" without the requisite investment for a stand-alone operation.

Schwab's OneSource

Charles Schwab & Company is the country's largest discount broker and is now offering a vehicle through commercial bank trust departments and money managers can increase their clients investment alternatives with nominal expense.

In mid-1992 Schwab introduced OneSource, a no-transaction-fee method for individuals and institutional investors to invest in no-load mutual funds. Schwab earns its fee, instead, from the mutual funds that are sold through OneSource, charging basis points on the assets brought into the mutual funds.

Schwab has now extended this service to small- and medium-sized institutional money managers that have had limited mobility among fund families because of cost constraints. The Institutional Mutual Fund OneSource is a combination of 258 no-load mutual funds from 27 fund families that are geared toward retail investors. Another 90 funds, including 35 no-load and 55 load funds, are from 17 fund families geared to investment managers and pension administrators. Institutional OneSource is ideal for the 401(k) market, bank trust departments, and investment managers.[5]

Schwab has adopted a client/server platform that incorporates SchwabLink, an electronic interface with client's PCs that has been instrumental in attracting institutional clientele. Each day, Schwab clients can down-load customer information for portfolio valuation. SchwabLink permits Schwab money management clients to post information directly to their respective customer records, saving the Schwab clients back-office time and expense. The 1,500 SchwabLink users represent 80% of all Schwab institutional investors.

Forming a strategic alliance with Schwab in the context of Institutional OneSource can vastly expand a bank's product offerings without any real additional cost. The benefit to the bank's retirement, trust, or investment customers is that a much wider range of mutual funds is available at low transactions costs. Daily valuations can be obtained easily and, each month, one efficient statement summarizes activity in all of the accounts.

Conclusion

Forming strategic alliances is but one way for a bank to increase its presence in the financial services industry. However, it can be an extremely efficient way to accomplish certain ultimate objectives. The key is to remain open to new ideas and to be willing to form alliances with individuals and companies that can add needed expertise.

Selected References

Allen, Paul H. *Reengineering the Bank: A Blueprint for Survival and Success*, Chicago: Probus Publishing, 1994.

Arend, Mark. "Tips for Technology Spending," *ABA Banking Journal*, August 1993, pp. 26–28.

Bird, Anat. "Banc One Centralizes Some Functions—Judiciously," *The American Banker*, October 19, 1994.

Borowsky, Mark. "Terminating the Paper Chase," *Bank Management*, April 1993, pp. 22–25.

Cantrell, Wanda and Mary Colby. "Getting a Grip on Information," *Bank Management*, September 1993, pp. 22–28.

Clark, David L. "Choosing Platform Automation Isn't For the Fainthearted," *ABA Banking Journal*, January 1993, pp. 56–60.

"Going to the Bank Electronically," *Independent Banker*, July 1994, pp. 38–40.

Johnson, Hazel J. *The New Global Banker: What Every U.S. Bank Must Know to Compete Internationally*, Chicago: Probus Publishing, 1994.

Lipin, Steven. "Eight Banks Form Clearinghouse to Cut Cost of Foreign-Exchange Transactions," *Wall Street Journal*, August 1, 1994, pp. A2 & A4.

Murphy, Patricia A. "Electronic Check Clearing Alternatives Take Shape," *ABA Banking Journal*, May 1993, pp. 62-73.

Murphy, Patricia A. "Using Imaging to Increase Check Shop Productivity," *Bank Management*, October 1993, pp. 54-55.

Radding, Alan. "Exploring Bank Technology's New Frontier (Oklahoma's Liberty Bancorp)," *Bank Management*, January 1993, pp. 43–46.

Radding, Alan. "Imaging Reaches a Threshold," *Bank Management*, March 1993, pp. 60–62.

Sellers, Rick. "Getting It Together in the Electronic Marketplace," *Bank Management*, January/February 1994, pp. 50–55.

"Shell Cuts Banks and Costs," *Corporate Finance*, December 1994, pp. 5–6.

Smith, Carrie R. "The Golden Touch (Charles Schwab & Co.)," *Wall Street & Technology*, vol. 12, no. 1, pp. 24–31.

Zecher, Joshua. "TCAM At Your Service," *Wall Street & Technology*, vol. 11, no. 13 (June 1994), pp. 16–20.

Endnotes

1   See *Reengineering the Bank: A Blueprint for Survival and Success*, pp. 231–248.

2   See "Shell Cuts Banks and Costs" in *Corporate Finance*, December 1994.

3   NASDAQ is an acronym for National Association of Securities Dealers Automated Quotation System.

4   Proof of deposit (POD) is the process of verifying the dollar amount on a check or draft that is included in a deposit. This verification is accomplished by comparing the handwritten amount on the check to the amount written on the deposit slip. POD is done after (1) the checks have been sorted by the sorter-reader into "on-us" and "on-others" categories and (2) the MICR line has been read to capture routing information and account numbers.

5   401(k) plans are employee savings plans that permit employees to contribute pre-tax amounts to an investment pool managed by the employer. These savings remain tax-deferred until withdrawal, but are subject to a penalty if withdrawn prior to the age of 59.5 years. Investors can place 401(k) assets into bank certificates of deposit, mutual funds, stocks, bonds, and other investment vehicles.

5

Valuation Techniques, Part I: The Balance Sheet

Introduction

The process of valuing a prospective merger partner or acquisition target involves both quantitative and qualitative issues. At the core of valuation lies the institution's balance sheet—the assets and liabilities that represent future cash flows. Increasingly, the rights and obligations that are not recorded on the balance sheet have assumed a more significant role—credit commitments, swaps, forward contracts, and other option-like instruments that often are collectively referred to as derivatives. At one time, noninterest income was composed primarily of service charges on deposits and trust fees. Now noninterest income is much more varied, including fees from brokerage activities, mutual fund sales, servicing assets after sales, and corporate finance. Arguably, off-balance sheet and fee-generating activities represent the greatest potential for growth in the banking industry and are vital parts of the valuation process. This chapter describes valuation techniques and then focuses on valuing the specific line items of the balance sheet. Chapter 6 describes the valuation of off-balance sheet items and fee income.

Valuation Approaches

For purposes of merger and acquisition, the price paid for a bank is often analyzed in terms of book value, assets minus liabilities—or more precisely, some multiple of book value. This section outlines several approaches to valuation, including their advantages and disadvantages:

- Discounted cash flow (DCF)
- P/E valuation
- Adjusted book value

Discounted Cash Flow (DCF)

The *discounted cash flow (DCF)* approach is the most theoretically valid approach because it considers future cash flow streams and the appropriate market rates to apply to them in determining their market value. This approach has been stipulated by the Financial Accounting Standards Board as the correct method of fair market valuation when objective quotations are unavailable.[1] In the application of DCF techniques to bank valuation, it is frequently assumed that earnings represent a good approximation of cash flow. A growth rate of earnings for the near term is also specified and earnings adjustments are made, as applicable. Examples of earnings adjustments include removing the effect of large amortizations of goodwill (from previous acquisitions) and reducing overly conservative provisions for loan loss.

The process of valuation often consists of the following steps:

1. Project earnings for each of the next five years, individually.
2. Find the present value of each year's earnings with the appropriate discount factor, using a weighted average cost of capital.
3. Apply a P/E ratio to the earnings in year 6 to establish the value of all earnings after year 5.
4. Find the present value of the result in step 2, using a discount factor for 5 years.

The advantage of this process is that it incorporates sound principles of financial theory with the use of present value factors. However, there are several disadvantages:

- The use of one discount rate assumes a constant capital structure and constant cost of capital. Actually, bank assets are financed with little permanent capital and considerable short-term liabilities in the form of bank deposits and short-term borrowed funds.
- The use of one growth rate for the earnings stream in the first five years assumes that the mix of business activities will remain the same. For example, the relative contributions

of income from loans and securities will
remain the same. However, a changing interest rate environment can have a significant
impact on the mix of loans vs. securities.

- Multiplying earnings in year 6 by a given P/E
  ratio is equivalent to dividing the earnings by
  the E/P ratio which, in turn, is equivalent to
  capitalizing the earnings at a rate of return that
  is required by equity holders in a no-growth
  scenario. Unless it is assumed that there will be
  no growth after year 5, this is inappropriate.

P/E Valuation

P/E valuation is a subset of the DCF process, as it is commonly applied. It involves:

1. Finding a comparable institution whose stock is
   publicly traded.
2. Determining the P/E ratio of the publicly traded
   institution.
3. Multiplying the earnings of the firm being analyzed by the P/E ratio of the publicly traded
   institution.

The approach is simple and intuitively appealing.
However, the disadvantages are several:

- As indicated above, application of this
  approach assumes no growth in earnings.
- If the stock in the bank being analyzed is not
  also publicly traded, its illiquidity will cause
  an over-valuation.

- It is difficult to find a comparable, publicly traded firm because of differences in competition, asset mix, management, and other variables.

Adjusted Book Value

The *adjusted book value* approach attempts to compensate for those factors that cause the book value of equity to differ from the market value. Book value is commonly adjusted by:

1. Subtracting intangibles.
2. Adding to the value of premises, as appropriate.
3. Reducing the allowance for loan loss when provisions have been overly conservative, to increase the value of the loan portfolio.
4. Reducing loans that appear not to be fully realizable (loan portfolio "haircuts").
5. Marking to market those securities that have not been recorded at market value.

This approach is useful, but can rarely be considered a complete valuation for several reasons:

- The impact of the interest rate environment on the value of loan and deposit portfolios is not addressed.
- Off-balance sheet positions are ignored.
- Fee-generating activities are not valued in any way.

Exhibit 5–1

Comparison of Industry Balance Sheet and Off-Balance Totals in 1993[1]

Balance Sheet Totals		% of Assets
Assets		
Cash and due from depository institutions	$273	7.4%
Investment securities	837	22.6
Temporary investments[2]	150	4.0
Loans and leases, net[3]	2,097	56.6
Assets held in trading accounts	122	3.3
Other assets	227	6.1
Total assets	$3,706	100.0%

Liabilities and Equity		
Deposits	$2,754	74.3%
Short-term borrowed funds[4]	496	13.4
Long-term borrowed funds[5]	39	1.1
Other liabilities[6]	120	3.2
Equity capital	297	8.0
Total liabilities and equity	$3,706	100.0%

Off-Balance Sheet Totals		% of Assets
Unused credit commitments[7]	$1,455	39.3%
Letters of credit[8]	191	5.2
Interest rate contracts[9]	5,573	150.4
Foreign exchange contracts[10]	3,975	107.2
Mortgages transferred with recourse[11]	5	0.1
Other off-balance sheet liabilities	96	2.6
Total off-balance sheet categories	$11,295	304.8%

Exhibit 5–1

Comparison of Industry Balance Sheet and Off-Balance Totals in 1993[1] (cont.)

1   Billions of dollars.

2   Federal funds sold and securities purchased under agreement to resell.

3   Net of allowance for losses and allocated transfer risk reserve ($53).

4   Federal funds purchased and securities sold under agreement to repurchase ($275), demand notes issued to the U.S. Treasury ($35), and other borrowed money ($186).

5   Mortgage indebtedness ($2) and subordinated notes and debentures ($37).

6   Includes limited-life preferred stock and related surplus.

7   Revolving lines secured by 1–4 family residential properties ($68); credit card lines ($660); commercial real estate, construction, and land development ($52); securities underwriting ($2); and all other ($673).

8   Financial standby letters of credit and foreign office guarantees ($117), performance standby letters of credit ($46), and commercial letters of credit ($28).

9   Notional amounts of swaps ($2,945); futures and forward contracts ($2,496); written options ($950), net of purchased options ($818).

10 Notional amounts of swaps ($277); spot, forward, and futures contracts ($3,689); written options ($263), net of purchased options ($255).

11 Amount of recourse exposure.

Source: FDIC Statistics on Banking, 1993.

Comprehensive Market Valuation

All of the above-mentioned approaches to bank valuation contribute to the assessment of a potential merger partner or acquisition target. However, no one of them gives a complete picture.

Exhibit 5–1 illustrates this point. Total banking industry assets in 1993 were $3.7 trillion, dominated primarily by loans (56.6%) and investment securities (22.6%). On the right hand side of the balance sheet, deposits dominated (74.3%). As of the same date, off-balance total reported to federal regulators amounted to $11.3 trillion or 304.8% of industry assets! Of this total, notional amounts of swaps (both interest rate and foreign exchange) represented $3.2 trillion. Yet even when these notional amounts are ignored, the net 1993 off-balance sheet exposure of the industry remains a staggering $8 trillion or 217.8% of industry assets. A comprehensive valuation approach cannot ignore off-balance sheet factors.

Exhibit 5–2 shows the significance of an analysis of noninterest income. In 1993, noninterest income was almost 31% of interest income, while noninterest expense was almost 57%. Interestingly, the breakdown of these categories is not well defined at the federal regulatory level. In noninterest income, $40 billion of the total $75 billion (53%) must be assigned to "all other" noninterest income. In noninterest expense, $63 billion of the total $139 billion (45%) is relegated to "all other." This suggests that the information-gathering function of federal regulators has not kept pace with the growth of the activities represented by these categories. Likewise, it is entirely possible that banking industry analysts have not refined the tools used to evaluate commercial bank prof-

Exhibit 5–2
Industry Income in 1993[1]

		% of Interest Income
Interest Income		
Loans	$175	71.4%
Lease financing receivables	3	1.2
Balances due from depository institutions	6	2.4
Investment securities	49	20.0
Assets held in trading accounts	7	2.9
Temporary investments[2]	5	2.1
Total interest income	245	100.0%
Interest Expense		
Deposits	<80>	<32.7>
Short-term borrowed funds[3]	<24>	<9.8>
Long-term borrowed funds[4]	<2>	<0.8>
Total interest expense	<106>	<43.3>
Net Interest Income	139	56.7
Provisions for loan loss	<17>	6.9
Net Interest Income, net of Provisions	122	49.8
Noninterest Income		
Fiduciary activities	11	4.5
Service charges and deposit accounts	15	6.1
Foreign exchange and transactions	3	1.2
Trading account gains and losses	6	2.4
All other noninterest income	40	16.3
Total noninterest income	75	30.6

Exhibit 5–2
Industry Income in 1993[1] (cont.)

Noninterest Expense

Salaries and employee benefits	<58>	<23.7>
Premises and equipment	<18>	<7.3>
All other noninterest expense	<u><63></u>	<u><25.7></u>
Total noninterest expense	<139>	<56.7>
Pre-tax net operating income	58	23.7
Gains on investment securities[5]	3	1.2
Income taxes	<20>	<8.2>
Extraordinary items, net of tax	<u>2</u>	<u>0.8</u>
Net Income	<u>$43</u>	17.6%

1 Billions of dollars.

2 Federal funds sold and securities purchased under agreements to resell.

3 Federal funds purchased and securities sold under agreements to repurchase ($9); demand notes issued to the U.S. Treasury, and other borrowed funds ($15).

4 Mortgage indebtedness and obligations under capitalized leases ($0.2), and subordinated notes and debentures ($2).

5 Not held in trading accounts.

Note: Percentages may not sum to the subtotals shown because of rounding differences.

Source: FDIC Statistics on Banking, 1993.

itability (and value) as it relates to those activities that are not based on the balance sheet. A comprehensive valuation approach must consider these areas explicitly.

Accordingly, the market valuation approach that will be described in this chapter and Chapter 6 incorporates all the relevant considerations, using discounted cash flow methodology:

- Balance sheet, including embedded options
- Off-balance positions
- Noninterest income and expense

Valuing the Balance Sheet

Market valuation models for bank assets and liabilities are based on time value of money concepts.[2] The exact specifications of a model, however, will depend on the characteristics of the particular financial instrument. In some cases, book value is a reasonable approximation of market value. For a few categories, professional appraisals are the best estimates. For those many categories of the balance sheet for which time value of money is appropriate the major parameters of market valuation models are:

- Future cash flows
- Time to maturity
- Appropriate discount rate

The basic model is:

$$MV = \sum_{t=1}^{n} \frac{CF_t}{(1+k)^t}$$

where MV = Market value

CF_t = Cash flow in year t

n = number of periods in the term of a fixed-income instrument

k = appropriate discount rate

This model may be applied to the following categories:

- Cash
- Temporary investments
- Investment securities
- Loans and lease financing
- Other assets
- Deposits
- Short-term borrowings
- Long-term borrowings

The market value of a bank's equity is the difference between the market value of assets and the market value of liabilities.

$$MV_E = MV_A - MV_L$$

where MV_E = Market value of equity

MV_A = Market value of assets

MV_L = Market value of liabilities

Cash

The *Cash* category includes:

- Vault cash
- Due from other banks

- Due from the Federal Reserve
- Cash items in collection

The balances in these accounts are funds that are available on a same-day or next-day basis. It is not necessary to apply valuation models to cash items. Market value is the same as book value.

Temporary Investments

Temporary Investments includes the following accounts:

- Interest-bearing time deposits in other banks
- Federal funds sold
- Term federal funds sold
- Securities purchased under agreement to resell

These are short-term instruments whose coupon (earning) rates and discount (market) rates will be similar. Thus, there will be little difference between market value and book value.

For *interest-bearing time deposits in other banks*, the appropriate model is:

$$MV = \frac{D(1+k_c)^n}{(1+k)^n}$$

where D = deposit amount

k_c = contractual (coupon) rate

k = appropriate discount rate

n = fraction of the year remaining before maturity

Consider an example in which the coupon rate equals the discount rate.

Assume: $D = \$100,000; k_c = .05; k = .05; n = .5.$

Result: $MV = 100,000(1.05)^{.5} / (1.05)^{.5}$

                                 $= 100,000$

Because the contractual (coupon) rate equals the market (discount) rate, the market value equals the book value.

The next example shows the effect on market value when the discount rate exceeds the contractual rate.

Assume: $D = \$100,000; k_c = .05; k = .055; n = .5.$

Result: $MV = 100,000(1.05)^{.5} / (1.055)^{.5}$

                                 $= 100,000(1.024695)/(1.027132)$

                                 $= 99,762.74$

The market value is lower than book value. Notice, however, that the difference is small, because the time to maturity is relatively short.

If the discount rate is less than the contractual rate, this relationship is reversed. Market value is greater than book value.

For *federal funds sold*, the appropriate model is similar to that for time deposits in other banks:

$$MV = \frac{FF(1+k_c)^n}{(1+k)^n}$$

where FF = amount of funds loaned

The most typical case is an overnight transaction for which there is no difference between contractual and market rates.

Assume: $\quad FF = 1,000,000; k_c = .04; k = .04; n = 1/365.$

Result: $\quad MV = 1,000,000(1.04)^{1/365}/(1.04)^{1/365}$

$$= 1,000,000$$

Term federal funds sold are slightly longer-term investments. Thus, the rate used to discount the cash flows will have a more significant impact on market value. However, these instruments are valued using the same model as the overnight transactions. The following is an example of a one-month contract:

Assume: $\quad FF = 1,000,000; k_c = .04; k = .045; n = 31/365.$

Result: $\quad MV = 1,000,000(1.04)^{31/365}/(1.045)^{31/365}$

$$= 1,000,000(1.003337)/(1.003745)$$
$$= 999,593.52$$

Note that there is still little difference between book and market values because of the short-term nature of the transaction.

For *securities purchased under agreement to resell,* the valuation model for these investments assumes that interest is earned on the securities while held by the bank.

$$MV = \sum_{t=1}^{n} \frac{CP_t}{\left(1+\dfrac{k}{m}\right)^t} + \frac{SP}{\left(1+\dfrac{k}{m}\right)^t}$$

where CP_t = coupon payment that the bank receives before resale

                    = $CR(M)/m$

           CR = coupon rate of securities purchased

           M = maturity value of securities purchased (also referred to as face value or par value)

          SP = selling price specified in resale agreement

            m = number of periods per year that interest is paid

             n = number of periods before resale

             k = appropriate discount rate

The following example assumes resale at a price other than maturity.

Assume: $SP = \$1,050,000; k = .045; n = one\ six\ month\ period;$
                 $m = 2; M = 1,000,000; CR = .05.$

Result: $CP_t = .05(1,000,000)/2$

               $= 25,000$

    $MV = 25,000/(1.0225) + 1,050,000/(1.0225)$

              $= 24,449.88 + 1,026,894.87$

              $= 1,051,334.75$

In this case, the interest to be earned increases the market value of the investment.

Investment Securities

The asset category of *investment securities* includes the following instruments:

- Treasury bills
- Treasury notes and bonds
- Government agency bonds
- Municipal bonds
- Zero-coupon bonds

These securities often have much longer maturities than temporary investments. Depending upon the interest rate environment, this can result in larger differences between book value and market value.

In the case of *Treasury bills (T-bills)*, the depth of the Treasury market means that market quotations are very easy to obtain. However, it is important to understand the mechanics of T-bill pricing. T-bills have an original maturity of less than one year with original maturities of 91 days, 182 days, and one year. These instruments will always sell below maturity value (with minimum denomination of $10,000) because they are discounted securities. That is, no interest is paid between the date of purchase and the maturity date.

$$MV = M - M(k)\left(\frac{N}{360}\right)$$

$$= M - D$$

where
M = maturity or face value
k = annual discount rate
N = number of days until maturity
D = discount from face value

$$= M(k)\left(\frac{N}{360}\right)$$

This example is a T-bill with an original maturity of six months purchased 82 days before the current date.

Assume: $M = 10,000; k = .04; N = 100.$

Result: $MV = 10,000 - 10,000(.04)(100/360)$

$= 10,000 - 111.11$

$= 9,888.89$

Treasury notes and bonds are longer-term securities, with notes having original maturities of two to 10 years and bonds 10 to 30 years. Original maturities for notes are 2, 3, 5, 7 and 10 years. Bonds are issued with 10-year and 30-year original maturities. Like Treasury bills, Treasury notes and bonds are traded in a well developed market. However, a significant difference is that the vast majority of these securities pay interest on a semiannual basis. The appropriate model values both the annuity of interest payments and the maturity value (minimum denomination of $1,000).

$$MV = \sum_{t=1}^{n} \frac{\left(\frac{(M)(CR)}{m}\right)}{\left(1+\frac{k}{m}\right)^{t}} + \frac{M}{\left(1+\frac{k}{m}\right)^{n}}$$

where
M = maturity or face value
CR = coupon rate
m = number of times per year interest is paid
= 2
$\frac{(M)(CR)}{m}$ = periodic (semiannual) interest payments

n = number of (semiannual) periods before maturity

k = annual discount rate

Consider the following Treasury note investment.

Assume: $M = 100,000; CR = .05; m = 2; k = .04; n = 6$ (3 *years*).

Note that the maturity date is exactly three years from the point of valuation (today).

Result:

$$MV = \left[\sum_{t=1}^{6} \left\{ (100,000)(.05)/2 \right\} /(1.02)^t \right]$$
$$+ \left[100,000/(1.02)^6 \right]$$
$$= \left[\sum_{t=1}^{6} 2,500/(1.02)^t \right]$$
$$+ \left[100,000/(1.02)^6 \right]$$
$$= 2,500 \left[\sum_{t=1}^{6} 1/(1.02)^t \right]$$
$$+ \left[100,000/(1.02)^6 \right]$$
$$= 2,500 \left(PVIFA_{.02,6} \right)$$
$$+ 100,000/1.126162$$
$$PVIFA_{.02,6} = (1/.02) \left(1 - \left\{ 1/(1.02)^6 \right\} \right)$$
$$= 5.601431$$
$$\therefore MV = 2,500 (5.601431) + 88,797.17$$
$$= 14,003.58 + 88,797.17$$
$$= 102,800.75$$

Exhibit 5–3
Bond Pricing Theorems

Bond Theorem #1

When the coupon rate equals the discount rate, a bond or note pays *exactly* the amount required by investors and its market value will equal par.

$$If\ CR = k,\ then\ MV = M$$

When the coupon rate equals the required return, the bond will sell at par value.

Bond Theorem #2

When the coupon rate is less than the discount rate, a bond pays *less than* the required amount and investors are not willing to pay the full face value for the bond.

$$If\ CR < k,\ then\ MV < M$$

When the coupon rate is less than the required return, the bond will sell at a discount.

Bond Theorem #3

When the coupon rate is greater than the discount rate, a bond pays *more than* investors require and the market is willing to pay a premium for it.

$$If\ CR > k,\ then\ MV > M$$

When the coupon rate is greater than the required return, the bond will sell at a premium.

Exhibit 5–3
Bond Pricing Theorems (cont.)

Bond Theorem #4

All other things being equal, the market value of a bond that is selling at a premium (discount) will decrease (increase) over time until
market value equals par value at the time of maturity.

All other things being equal, the market value of a bond will
approach its face value as the maturity date approaches.

Bond Theorem #5

In general, the higher the discount rate used, the lower the price.
The lower the discount rate used, the higher the price.

There is an inverse relationship between changes in the discount
rate and changes in the price of a bond.

Legend:

CR	Coupon rate
k	Discount or market rate (required rate of return)
M	Maturity value
MV	Market value

The market value of these notes is $102,800.75. The
market quotation will not be this exact amount because
prices are stated as dollars and 32nds of a dollar per $100
of face value. Thus, the market quotation for these notes
will be between 102.25 or $102,781.25 (25/36 = .78125)
and 102.26 or $102,812.50 (26/32 = .8125). Notice too that
market value is higher than par value because the
coupon rate exceeds the required return. If the coupon

rate were less than the required return, the market value would be less than par value. [See Exhibit 5–3 for a summary of bond pricing theorems.]

Now consider the example of Treasury bonds that are being valued at a date that is not exactly one period before the next coupon payment. The following valuation model adjusts for this situation:

$$MV = \left(\sum_{t=1}^{n+(1-p)} \frac{\left(\frac{(M)(CR)}{m} \right)}{\left(1+\frac{k}{m}\right)^t} \right)\left(1+\frac{k}{m}\right)^{1-p} + \frac{M}{\left(1+\frac{k}{m}\right)^n} + \frac{(M)(CR)}{m}(1-p)$$

where p = partial period until next interest payment

= (number of days before next interest payment)/(total number of days per period)

n = total number of periods before maturity, including full periods and partial period

$(1-p)$ = partial period that has elapsed since last interest payment

$\left[\frac{(M)(CR)}{m} \right](1-p)$ = interest accrued since last interest payment

Notice that the present value of the interest payments is computed for a whole number of periods—(n + (1–p)). That is, the present value of the interest payments is computed using a point of valuation that is immediately following the last interest payment, or (1–p) peri-

Exhibit 5–4
Treasury Notes with Three Years to Maturity
Valued Between Coupon Dates

Date

Jan. 1 1996	Feb. 15 1996	Aug. 15 1996	Feb. 15 1997	Aug. 15 1997	Feb. 15 1998	Aug. 15 1998

Time Line

0	.25	1.25	2.25	3.25	4.25	5.25
	2,500	2,500	2,500	2,500	2,500	2,500
						100,000

Note: Time line describes $100,000 in 5 percent U.S. Treasury notes that pay interest semiannually and mature in two years, 7.5 months (5.25 semiannual periods).

ods ago. Using this point of valuation makes it possible to use PVIFA factors for an integer (not fractional) number of periods and to correctly value all of the remaining interest payments. However, this valuation is valid only for $(1-p)$ periods ago. To value these cash flows on the current date (time zero), it is necessary to compound the annuity results for $(1-p)$ periods.

Exhibit 5-4 illustrates an example of a security being valued between coupon dates. The point of valuation (POV) is January 1, 1996, while the next coupon payment will be made 45 days later on February 15. Because the maturity date is August 15, 1998, the time to maturity for these notes is two years and 7.5 months.

Assume: $M = 100,000; CR = .05; m = 2; k = .04; n = 5.25$

$p = 45/182 = .24725 \cong .25; (1-p) = (1-.25) = .75.$

Result:

$$MV = \left[\sum_{t=1}^{(5.25+.75)} 2500/(1.02)^t \right] \left[(1.02)^{.75} \right]$$

$$+ \left[100,000/(1.02)^{5.25} \right]$$

$$+ \left[(100,000)(.05)/2 \right] (.75)$$

$$= 2,500 \left(PVIFA_{.02,6} \right) (1.0149628)$$

$$+ 100,000/1.1095603$$

$$+ 2,500(.75)$$

$$PVIFA_{.02,6} = (1/.02) \left(1 - \left\{ 1/(1.02)^6 \right\} \right)$$

$$= 5.6014309$$

$$\therefore MV = 2,500(5.6014309)(1.0149628)$$

$$+ 90,125.79 + 1,875$$

$$= 14,213.11 + 90,125.79 + 1,875$$

$$= 106,213.90$$

When the POV occurs between coupon payments, the market value includes the present value of future cash flows—adjusted for the partial period—and the interest already accrued.

Government agency bonds fall into two basic categories:

- pass-through certificates
- mortgage-backed bonds

Generally, market quotations for government agency securities are readily available. Both types are mortgage-related. However, their valuation is based on different patterns of cash flow.

Holders of *pass-through securities* receive a proportional share of the principal and interest payments from the underlying mortgages. Conceptually, this is equivalent to receiving an annuity. The actual term over which payments are received will not be the remaining time to maturity of the underlying mortgages, however. Mortgages are refinanced when market interest rates decline significantly and when the existing homes are sold to purchase new homes. As a result, the average term of a government agency security is typically less than 15 years.

The risk of prepayment is an important element in the market valuation of these securities. One approach to compensate for this risk is to increase the discount rate used, effectively reducing the market value. This is the approach that is used in this section. Another adjustment for prepayment, covered in a later section entitled "Embedded Options," is to place a value on the embedded prepayment option by estimating prepayments.

Valuation is accomplished by determining the implied amount of monthly payments and discounting the value of this annuity at the appropriate discount rate.

$$MV = \sum_{t=1}^{n} \frac{CF_t}{\left(1+\dfrac{k}{m}\right)^t}$$

where CF_t = implied monthly payment of interest and principal

                n = number of months before maturity

                m = number of times per year payments are made

                  = 12

                k = appropriate discount rate

The appropriate discount rate should be related to other long-term yields, that is, bond yields. There is a difference in the frequency of payments between these two instruments, however. Bonds generally pay semiannual interest while mortgage pass-throughs pay monthly. As a result, a lower required rate on the mortgage will provide the same effective return as the bond.

$$k_{EPT} = \left(1 + \frac{k_{PC}}{12}\right)^{12} - 1$$

where k_{EPT} = effective pass-through yield
                k_{PT} = stated pass-through yield

In making this conversion, the first step is to establish the appropriate bond yield, the minimum acceptable yield for the given class of pass-through securities. This bond yield is then set equal to the effective pass-through yield and the equation is solved for the stated pass-through return. For example, suppose that an investor seeks the equivalent of a bond yield of 10.47 percent. Substituting this into the equation for effective pass-through yield.

$$.1047 = \left(1 + k_{PT}/12\right)^{12} - 1$$

$$1.1047 = \left(1 + k_{PT}/12\right)^{12}$$

$$1.1047^{1/12} = \left(1 + k_{PT}/12\right)$$

$$12\left(1.1047^{1/12} - 1\right) = k_{PT}$$

$$= .10$$

In the following example, the required return has been adjusted in this way.

Suppose that a bank holds a portfolio of government agency pass-through securities with a face value of $1,000,000.

Assume: $M = 1,000,000; CR = .08; m = 12; k = .10;$

$n = 360 = 12$ *payments per year for 30 years.*

(Notice that the 10 percent discount rate is substantially higher than the coupon rate to compensate for prepayment risk.)

The first step is to determine the implied monthly payment which will cause the present value of future cash flows to exactly equal $1,000,000 when using the 8 percent coupon rate.[3]

Result:

$$1,000,000 = CF_t\left(PVIFA_{(.08/12),360}\right)$$

$$CF_t = 1,000,000 / \left(PVIFA_{(.08/12),360}\right)$$

$$PVIFA_{(.08/12),360} = \left(1/(.08/12)\right)\left(1 - \left\{1/\left(1+.08/12\right)^{360}\right\}\right)$$

$$= \left(1/.006667\right)\left(1 - \left\{1/\left(1.006667\right)^{360}\right\}\right)$$

$$= 136.2783152$$

$$CF_t = 1,000,000 / 136.2783152$$

$$= 7,337.92$$

The market value of the securities is the present value of these implied monthly payments of $7,337.92 at the discount rate of 10 percent.

$$MV = \sum_{t=1}^{360} 7,337.92 / \left(1+.10/12\right)^t$$

$$= \left(7,337.92\right)\sum_{t=1}^{360} 1/\left(1.008333\right)^t$$

$$= \left(7,337.92\right)\left(PVIFA_{.008333,360}\right)$$

$$PVIFA_{.008333,360} = \left(1/.0083333\right)\left(1 - \left\{1/\left(1.0083333\right)^{360}\right\}\right)$$

$$= 113.9512038$$

$$MV = 7,337.92\left(113.9512038\right)$$

$$= 836,164.82$$

On the other hand, *mortgage-backed bonds* do not pay the principal and interest from the underlying mortgages. Instead, the bonds are collateralized by the mort-gages, but pay interest and maturity value much like a Treasury or corporate bond. Because of this, the model for market valuation is the same as the model for Treasury bonds.

Municipal bonds are also valued in the same way as Treasury bonds. One important difference, however, is the required rate of return. Because the interest income from municipal bonds is exempt from federal taxation, the required return is lower than for Treasury bonds. Another important distinction is that some municipal bonds are callable, that is, can be redeemed by the issuer prior to the original maturity date. The call feature is essentially an option owned by the bond issuer. The value of this embedded option is discussed in the later section entitled "Embedded Options."

The model for noncallable bonds and for bonds for which there has already been an advance refunding is the same as for Treasury notes and bonds.

$$MV = \sum_{t=1}^{n} \frac{\left(\frac{(M)(CR)}{m}\right)}{\left(1+\frac{k}{m}\right)^t} + \frac{M}{\left(1+\frac{k}{m}\right)^n}$$

Suppose that municipal bonds issued five years ago have 15 years remaining to maturity.

Assume: $M = 50,000; CR = .07; m = 4; k = .05; n = 60.$

$$MV = \sum_{t=1}^{60} \{(50,000)(.07)/4\}/(1.0125)^t$$

$$+\left[50,000/(1.0125)^{60}\right]$$

$$= 875\left(PVIFA_{.0125,60}\right) + 50,000/2.107181$$

$$PVIFA_{.0125,60} = (1/.0125)\left(1 - \left\{1/(1.0125)^{60}\right\}\right)$$

$$MV = 875(42.03459179) + 23,728.38$$

$$= 36,780.27 + 23,728.38$$

$$= 60,508.65$$

Now suppose that the municipal bonds that were issued five years ago are callable and that the bonds have call protection for a total of ten years or another five years from now (time 0). If called in year 6, the bonds will be redeemed at 103, that is, for par value plus a call premium of 3. Because market interest rates are low, the bond issuers have structured an advance refunding. That is, new bonds have already been issued and the proceeds placed in trust until the first call date five years from now. The valuation model reflects these circumstances.

$$MV = \sum_{t=1}^{c} \frac{\left(\dfrac{(M)(CR)}{m}\right)}{\left(1 + \dfrac{k}{m}\right)^t} + \frac{CP}{\left(1 + \dfrac{k}{m}\right)^c}$$

where $\quad c\ =\ $ number of periods before the first call date

$CP\ =\ $ call price on first call date

Assume: $\quad M = 50,000; CR = .07; m = 4; k = .05; n = 60;$
$c = 20; CP = 51,500\ (103\%\ of\ face\ value).$

Result:
$$MV = \sum_{t=1}^{20}\left\{(50,000)(.07)/4\right\}/(1.0125)^t$$
$$+\left[51,500/(1.0125)^{20}\right]$$
$$= 875\left(PVIFA_{.0125,20}\right)+51,500/1.282037$$
$$PVIFA_{.0125,40} = (1/.0125)\left(1-\left\{1/(1.0125)^{20}\right\}\right)$$
$$= 17.599316$$
$$\therefore\ MV = 875(17.599316)+40,170.45$$
$$= 55,569.85$$

Under an advance refunding, the market value of municipal bonds is generally lower than it would be otherwise because of the shortened life of the instruments. As shown in this example, this is true even when the bonds will be called at a premium.

Zero-coupon bonds do not pay interim interest payments before maturity. The only relevant cash flow is the final pay-off of the maturity value.

$$MV = \frac{M}{(1+k)^n}$$

where M = maturity value

             n = number of years until maturity

The value of the bond is the present value of the maturity value. Accordingly, these bonds will always have a market value that is less than face value. For example:

Assume: $M = 100,000; k = .05; n = 10.$

Result: $MV = 100,000\left(1/\left(1.05\right)^{10}\right)$

$$= 100,000\left(.613913\right)$$

$$= 61,391.33$$

Loans

Readily available market quotations exist for many investment securities. However, for the loan portfolio, usually representing an even larger investment than the investment portfolio, there is less available market information. This section contains market models for the following categories:

- Commercial loans
- Mortgage loans
- Consumer installment loans
- Lease financing
- Nonaccrual loans

The terms of *commercial loans* vary significantly but most can be described with one of the following general cash flow patterns:

- bullet loans
- working capital lines of credit
- term loans

Bullet loans require no payment of interest or principal until the loan matures. The market value of these loans is the present value of the future pay-off of interest and principal.

$$MV = \frac{L\left(1+\dfrac{k_L}{m}\right)^n}{\left(1+\dfrac{k}{m}\right)^n}$$

where

L = loan amount

k_L = loan rate

n = number of periods before loan matures

m = number of times per year interest is compounded

Consider a bullet loan with quarterly compounding.

Assume: $L = 250,000; k_L = .075; m = 4; k = .08; n = 20$ *(five years)*.

Result: $MV = 250,000(1+.075/4)^{20}/(1+.08/4)^{20}$

$= 250,000(1.449948)/(1.485947)$

$= 243,943.42$

Working capital lines of credit are arrangements that involve a loan amount that will change. At any point in time, however, the value of a portfolio of lines of credit must be based on actual borrowings outstanding and an estimate of when these balances will be repaid. These estimates are most appropriately based on past experience with the credit lines. In addition to normal interest payments, commitment fees are assessed on unused portions of the lines. These fees are usually stated in terms of percent per annum, as are interest rates. The valuation model considers both the borrowings and the unused portion of the line.

$$MV = \frac{A(1+k_{LC})^n + (MX - A)\left((1+k_{CF})^n - 1\right)}{(1+k)^n}$$

where
$$\begin{aligned}
A &= \text{actual borrowings to date} \\
MX &= \text{maximum credit available} \\
k_{LC} &= \text{interest rate on borrowings} \\
k_{CF} &= \text{commitment fee} \\
n &= \text{average maturity of lines of credit} \\
&\quad\ \text{or average time before they are} \\
&\quad\ \text{expected to be paid off}
\end{aligned}$$

Consider a portfolio of credit lines that have an average maturity of nine months.

Assume: $A = 2,000,000; MX = 5,000,000; k_{LC} = .10;$
$k_{CF} = .01; k = .105; n = .75$

Result:

$$MV = \begin{bmatrix} 2,000,000(1.10)^{.75} \\ +(5,000,000 - 2,000,000) \\ \left((1.01)^{.75} - 1\right) \end{bmatrix} / (1.105)^{.75}$$

$$= \begin{bmatrix} (2,000,000)(1.0740995) \\ +(3,000,000)(.0074907) \end{bmatrix} / (1.0777591)$$

$$= 2,014,059.64$$

Term loans are extended for periods of time in excess of one year. They may be structured in one of two formats:

- installment loans
- interest-only loans

The market value of an *installment loan* is the present value of the payment annuity. The amount of the payment for a given loan is determined by the contractual loan rate and time to maturity.

$$MV = \left(\frac{L}{PVIFA_{\left(\frac{k_L}{m},n\right)}} \right)\left(PVIFA_{\left(\frac{k}{m},n\right)} \right)$$

where $\quad L$ = loan amount

$\quad m$ = number of times per year that payments are made

$\quad n$ = number of periods before maturity

$\dfrac{L}{PVIFA\left(\dfrac{k}{m},n\right)}$ = periodic loan payments

Consider a three-year loan with quarterly payments.

Assume: $\quad L = 1,000,000; k_L = .11; k = .105; m = 4; n = 12.$

Result:

$$MV = \left[1,000,000 / PVIFA_{.11/4,12}\right]\left[PVIFA_{.105/4,12}\right]$$

$$PVIFA_{.11/4,12} = \left(1/(.11/4)\right)\left(1 - \left\{1/(1+.11/4)^{12}\right\}\right)$$

$$= (36.363636)(1-.7221344)$$

$$= 10.10420354$$

$$PVIFA_{.105/4,12} = \left(1/(.105/4)\right)\left(1 - \left\{1/(1+.105/4)^{12}\right\}\right)$$

$$= (38.0952381)(1-.732760345)$$

$$= 10.18055829$$

$$MV = \left[1,000,000/10.10420354\right]\left[10.18055829\right]$$

$$= 1,007,556.73$$

The market value of an *interest-only loan* is the value of the interest payments and the pay-off at the end of the term. Thus, this type of loan is valued in the same way as an interest-paying bond.

$$MV = L\left(\frac{k_L}{m}\right)\left(PVIFA_{\left(\frac{k}{m},n\right)}\right) + \frac{L}{\left(1+\dfrac{k}{m}\right)^n}$$

where $\quad L\left(\dfrac{k_L}{m}\right) = \quad$ periodic interest payment

Consider a three-year loan that compounds interest semiannually.

Assume: $\qquad L = 1,000,000; k_L = .11; k = .105; m = 2; n = 6.$

Result:

$$MV = \left[1,000,000(.11/2)\left(PVIFA_{.105/2,6}\right)\right]$$
$$+ \left[1,000,000/(1+.105/2)^6\right]$$

$$PVIFA_{.105/2,6} = \left(1/.105/2\right)\left(1-\left\{1/(1+.105/2)^6\right\}\right)$$
$$= (19.047619)(1-.73564345)$$
$$= 5.0353628$$
$$MV = \left[(55,000)(5.0353628)\right]+735,643.45$$
$$= 1,012,588.40$$

A portfolio of term loans must be separated into the two classifications of installment and interest-only loans before they can be correctly valued because their cash flow patterns are significantly different. Once this is accomplished, each classification may be analyzed in terms of total balance, average loan rate, and average time to maturity.

Mortgage loans are long-term loans secured by real estate. Both residential and commercial mortgage loans are governed by the same principles of market valuation. However, the two types of mortgages should be kept separate because they have significantly different risk profiles which will affect the selection of discount rate. Within each of the two categories, subgrouping should include loans with common characteristics. The four subgroups are:

- fixed-rate mortgages
- adjustable rate mortgages (ARMs)
- graduated payment mortgages (GPMs)
- balloon mortgages

Fixed-rate mortgages typically have an original maturity of 25 to 30 years. The market value of a portfolio of these loans will depend on the implied periodic (usually monthly) payment and the average time to maturity.

$$MV = \left(\frac{L}{PVIFA_{\left(\frac{k_L}{m},n\right)}} \right)\left(PVIFA_{\left(\frac{k}{m},n\right)} \right)$$

where $\dfrac{L}{PVIFA\left(\frac{k_L}{m},n\right)}$ = implied periodic payment based on the loan amount (L) and the contractual mortgage rate

Suppose a mortgage is to be repaid in monthly installments over 25 years:

Assume: $L = 150,000; k_m = .10; k = .08; n = 300.$

Result: $MV = \left(150,000 / PVIFA_{.10/12,300}\right)\left(PVIFA_{.08/12,300}\right)$

$$PVIFA_{.10/12,300} = \left(1/.0083333\right)\left[1 - \left\{1/\left(1.0083333\right)^{300}\right\}\right]$$

$$= \left(120\right)\left(1 - .0829406\right)$$

$$= 110.047128$$

$$PVIFA_{.08/12,300} = \left(1/.0066667\right)\left[1 - \left\{1/\left(1.0066667\right)^{300}\right\}\right]$$

$$= \left(149.999\right)\left(1 - .1362352\right)$$

$$= 129.5638562$$

$$MV = \left[150,000 / 110.047128\right]\left[129.5638562\right]$$

$$= 176,602.32$$

If the borrower decides to prepay this mortgage, however, its market value will not be $176,602.32. The same principle applies as with the advance refunding of a municipal bond. If the mortgage is repaid prior to the original maturity date, its market value will decline. Unlike the case of advance refunding, the bank does not know whether this particular loan will be prepaid. The borrower owns an option to prepay but is not obligated to do so. The value of this option is described in a later section entitled "Embedded Options."

Adjustable-rate mortgages (ARMs) will pay interest that varies with market interest rates. The rate adjustments are often made twice a year. As a result, the market value of a portfolio of ARMs will be close to book value because the loan (coupon) rate will be close to the market (required) rate.

These rate adjustments cause ARMs to be less subject to prepayments that are motivated by interest rate changes. However, if the loan contract includes interest rate caps (ceiling—maximum rate, floor—minimum rate, or collar—cap and floor), these provisions constitute options owned either by the borrower or by the bank. These options are also evaluated in the later section "Embedded Options."

Graduated payment mortgages (GPMs) are primarily fixed-rate instruments. GPMs allow the borrower to make smaller payments in the early years of the loan. Typically, payments increase over the first five to ten years and then level off to a constant payment thereafter. During the early years, the payment reductions are added to the unpaid balance. The market valuation of GPMs depends on the precise cash flow stream to the bank. Thus, the actual payments must be analyzed.

$$MV = \sum_{t=1}^{g} \frac{\left(\dfrac{L}{PVIFA_{\left(\frac{k_L}{m},n\right)}} - PR_t \right)}{\left(1+\dfrac{k}{m}\right)^t}$$

$$+ \frac{\left(\left(\dfrac{L}{PVIFA_{\left(\frac{k}{m},n\right)}} \right)\left(PVIFA_{\left(\frac{k}{m},n-g\right)} \right) + \sum_{t=1}^{g} PR_t \right)}{PVIFA_{\left(\frac{k}{m},n-g\right)}}$$

$$* \left(PVIFA_{\left(\frac{k}{m},n-g\right)} \right) * \left(\dfrac{1}{\left(1+\dfrac{k}{m}\right)^g} \right)$$

where

n	=	total number of payments
m	=	number of payments per year
g	=	periods with graduated payments
PR_t	=	payment reduction in period t

$$\dfrac{L}{PVIFA\left(\frac{k}{m},n\right)}$$ = normal monthly payment

$$\left(\dfrac{L}{PVIFA_{\left(\frac{k}{m},n\right)}} \right)\left(PVIFA_{\left(\frac{k}{m},n-g\right)} \right)$$ = unpaid loan balance after g periods under the normal amortization schedule

$$\sum_{t=1} PR_t = \text{total amount of payment reductions to be added to unpaid balance at period } g$$

The following example illustrates the stages of this valuation process by analyzing:

- the normal amortization schedule
- the amount of negative amortization during the early years
- the necessary payment during the later years
- the present value of all payments

Assume: $L = 150,000; k_m = .10; k = .08; m = 12; n = 300;$

monthly PR = 250 in year 1, 200 in year 2,

150 in year 3, 100 in year 4, and 50 in year 5.[4]

The normal monthly payment for this loan is $1,363.05.

$$L = Pymt\left[\left(1/\left(k_m / m\right)\right)\left(1 - \left\{1/\left(1 + k_m / m\right)^n\right\}\right)\right]$$

$$150,000 = Pymt\left[110.47128\right]$$

$$1,363.05 = Pymt$$

Exhibit 5–5 shows the loan balance at the end of each year under the normal amortization schedule. These balances are computed as the present value of the remaining payments at the end of each year. Under the normal amortization schedule, the unpaid balance declines from $150,000 at time 0 to $141,245.54 by the end of year 5.

The graduated payments are lower than $1,363.05, however. Each of the first year's payments is $1,113.05

Exhibit 5–5
Graduated Payment Mortgage Normal
Amortization First 60 Payments

End of Year	Present Value of Remaining Payments	Unpaid Balance
0		$150,000.00
1	$1363.05(PVIFA_{10/12,288}) = 1363.05(109.005045)$	148,579.33
2	$1363.05(PVIFA_{10/12,276}) = 1363.05(107.85337295)$	147,010.03
3	$1363.05(PVIFA_{10/12,264}) = 1363.05(106.5818563)$	145,276.40
4	$1363.05(PVIFA_{10/12,252}) = 1363.05(105.1768013)$	143,361.24
5	$1363.05(PVIFA_{10/12,240}) = 1363.05(103.6246187)$	141,245.54

Note: Exhibit represents the normal amortization of a 25-year, $150,000 mortgage during the first five years. Monthly payments are based on a mortgage loan rate of 10 percent:

$$PV = Pymt\left[\left(1/(k_m/m)\right)\left(1-\left\{1/(1+k_m/m)^n\right\}\right)\right]$$

where k_m = mortgage loan rate = .10

m = payments per year = 12

$150,000 = Pymt[110.047128]$

$1363.05 = Pymt$

Exhibit 5–6
Graduated Payment Mortgage Negative
Amortization First 60 Payments

	Balance under Normal amortization		Negative Amortization	New
Year	Beginning	Ending	During year[1]	Balance[2]
0		150,000.00		
1	150,000.00	148,579.33	3,000	151,579.33
2	148,579.33	147,010.03	2,400	152,410.03
3	147,010.03	145,276.40	1,800	152,476.40
4	145,276.40	143,361.24	1,200	151,761.24
5	143,361.24	141,245.54	600	150,245.54
			9,000	

1 The normal payment is reduced by a flat amount each month during the first 60 months:

Year	Monthly Reduction
1	$250
2	200
3	150
4	100
5	50

2 The new balance under negative amortization equals the ending balance under normal amortization plus the cumulative payment reductions.

($1,363.05–$250) and each payment in the second year is $1,163.05 ($1,363.05–$200). The payments increase by $50 each year so that the monthly payment in year 5 is $1,313.05. This is a total of $9,000 in payment reductions, or negative amortization, over the five-year period.

Exhibit 5–6 shows how the loan balance increases to $150,245.54 by the end of year 5. This amount must be amortized over the remaining 240 months.

$$PV = Pymt\left(PVIFA_{k/m,n}\right)$$
$$Pymt = PV / \left(PVIFA_{k/m,n}\right)$$
$$= 150,245.54 / PVIFA_{.10/12,240}$$
$$= 150,245.54 / 103.624619$$
$$= 1,449.90$$

The market value of this loan is the present value of the first 60 payments plus the present value of the 240 at $1,449.90 each.

$$PV_{240\ payments} = 1,449.90\left(PVIFA_{.08/12,240}\right)$$
$$= 1,449.90\left(119.554292\right)$$
$$= 173,341.77$$

Because the first payment in this annuity occurs in period 61, the point of valuation is period 60.[5] Thus, the $173,341.77 must be discounted for 60 periods to time 0.

Exhibit 5–7

Graduated Payment Mortgage Present
Value of First 60 Payments

Year	Monthly Payment	Pymt (PVIFA)[1]	POV[2]	PVIF[3]	Present Value of Payments[4]
1	1,113.05	12,795.38	0	1.0000000	12,795.38
2	1,163.05	13,370.17	12	.9233615	12,345.50
3	1,213.05	13,944.96	24	.8525964	11,889.42
4	1,263.05	14,519.75	36	.7872546	11,430.74
5	1,313.05	15,094.54	48	.7269206	10,972.53
					59,433.57

1 Factor is computed for the combination of 8 percent and 12 periods.

2 Point of valuation (POV) for a present value annuity factor is one period before the first cash flow in the annuity.

3 Factor is computed for the combination of 8 percent and the number of periods between the POV and time 0.

4 Value of the payments at time 0 is the product of the present value of the annuity (Pymt(PVIFA)) and the present value interest factor of a single amount (PVIF).

$$PV = 173,341.77\left(1/\left(1+.08/12\right)^{60}\right)$$
$$= 173,341.77\left(.67121043\right)$$
$$= 116,348.80$$

The present value of the first 60 payments must be added to this amount. Exhibit 5–7 shows that the value of these payments at time 0 is $59,433.57. The value of this loan is, therefore, $175,782.37.

$$MV = 59,433.57 + 116,348.80$$
$$= 175,782.37$$

Valuing a portfolio of graduated payment loans will require an assessment of the payments to be received during the negative amortization period and the payments that are scheduled after the negative amortization period. This is best accomplished by separating the loans that are still in the negative amortization phase from those that have reached the stable payment phase.

Balloon mortgages are shorter-term loans that require a large payment at the end of the term of the loan. Generally, the two types of balloon mortgages are:

- interest-only loans
- amortizing loans

Interest-only balloon mortgage loans are similar to bonds that pay interest during the life of the loan and the entire principal at the end of the term.

$$MV = \frac{(L)\left(\frac{k_m}{m}\right)}{PVIFA_{\left(\frac{k_L}{m},n\right)}} + \frac{L}{\left(1+\frac{k}{m}\right)^n}$$

where L = loan amount

$(L)\left(\frac{k_m}{m}\right)$ = periodic interest payment

An example of annual interest payments illustrates this application.

Assume: $L = 100,000; k_m = .09; k = .095; m = 1; n = 5.$

Result: $MV = 100,000(.09)\left(PVIFA_{.095,5}\right)$

$$+ 100,000\left(1/(1.095)^5\right)$$

$$= 9,000(3.839709)$$

$$+ 100,000(.6352277)$$

$$= 34,557.38 + 63,522.77$$

$$= 98,080.15$$

On the other hand, the payments for an *amortizing balloon mortgage loan* are established as if the loan will be repaid over a longer period of time, perhaps 30 years, but the balance is due after a shorter period of time.

$$MV = \left(\frac{L}{PVIFA_{\left(\frac{k_L}{m},n\right)}}\right)\left(PVIFA_{\left(\frac{k}{m},b\right)}\right) + \frac{B}{\left(1 + \frac{k}{m}\right)^b}$$

where

n = number of periods over which the interim payments are set up

$\dfrac{L}{PVIFA_{\left(\frac{k_L}{m},n\right)}}$ = periodic payment of interest and principal

b = number of periods that will elapse before the date of the balloon payment

B = amount of the balloon payment

$$= \left(\frac{L}{PVIFA_{\left(\frac{k_L}{m},n\right)}} \right) \left(PVIFA_{\left(\frac{k}{m},n-b\right)} \right)$$

= value of the remaining payments

In some cases, the loan rate may be set below market for this type of loan because of the early pay-off. The market value of the loan will be the present value of the periodic payments and the balloon payment.

Consider the a set up to be amortized over 30 years with a balloon payment after year 5.

Assume: $L = 100,000; k_m = .07; k = .095; n = 360; b = 60.$

Result: $Monthly\ payment = 100,000 / PVIFA_{(.07/12),360}$

$$= 100,000 / 150.307568$$

$$= 665.30$$

$$PV\ of\ payments = 665.30 \left(PVIFA_{(.095/12),60} \right)$$

$$= 665.30 \left(47.614827 \right)$$

$$= 31,678.14$$

$$B = 665.30 \left(PVIFA_{.07/12,300} \right)$$

$$= 665.30 \left(141.486903 \right)$$

$$= 94,131.24$$

$$PV\ of\ B = 94,131.24 / \left(1 / \left(1 + .095/12 \right)^{60} \right)$$

$$= 94,131.24 \left(.6230493 \right)$$

$$= 58,648.40$$

$$MV = 31,678.14 + 58,648.40$$

$$= 90,326.54$$

When valuing a portfolio of balloon mortgages, it is necessary to determine the total loan amount, the average loan (coupon) rate, and the average loan term over which the payments have been set up. This information will form the basis of the estimate of the periodic payment. These implied payments will be received until the average date of balloon payment. The implied payments should then be discounted at the market rate. The average balloon payment is the value of the remaining payments as of the balloon payment date. This average must then also be discounted to time 0.

These valuation approaches for mortgage loans are cost-effective and theoretically sound. The loans in each category have similar characteristics with respect to cash flow pattern and as long as the residential mortgages are separated from the commercial portfolio, differences in risk characteristics are minimized.

The most common type of consumer installment loan is an automobile loan. These loans are valued as annuities in the same way as fixed-rate mortgage loans. The valuation model is:

$$MV = \left(\frac{L}{PVIFA_{\left(\frac{k_L}{m}, n \right)}} \right) \left(PVIFA_{\left(\frac{k}{m}, n \right)} \right)$$

The following is an example of a four-year loan with monthly payments.

Assume: $L = 20,000; k_L = .15; k = .13; n = 48.$

Result: $MV = \left(20,000 / PVIFA_{(.15/12),48}\right)\left(PVIFA_{(.13/12),48}\right)$

$= \left(20,000 / 35.9314809\right)\left(37.2751898\right)$

$= \left(556.61\right)\left(37.2751898\right)$

$= 20,747.74$

Consumer installment loans are subject to prepayment risk but not to the same extent as mortgage loans because consumer installment borrowers are less interest-rate-sensitive than mortgage borrowers.

Lease financing is similar to purchase financing with the exception that the borrower must pay a residual value at the end of the term of the lease to obtain ownership of the asset. Commercial leases should be separated from consumer leases for purposes of market valuation because the collateral and risk profiles of portfolios may be quite different. Once separated, however, the principles of market valuation are the same.

The residual value is similar to a balloon payment in a mortgage. The difference is that the residual is not a legal obligation of the borrower. At the end of the lease, the borrower may elect to not pay the residual and relinquish possession of the asset. Because the bank would then sell the asset, it is vital that the residual used for valuation purposes be a realistic estimate of the fair market value at the end of the lease term.

The market value of a lease is the present value of lease payments plus the present value of the residual.

$$MV = \left(\frac{L}{PVIFA_{\left(\frac{k_L}{m},n \right)}} \right) \left(PVIFA_{\left(\frac{k}{m},n \right)} \right) + \frac{R}{\left(1 + \frac{k}{m} \right)^n}$$

where

L = loan amount

= amount to be amortized

$\dfrac{L}{PVIFA\left(\frac{k_L}{m},n \right)}$ = periodic payment of interest and principal

R = residual value

Consider the lease for a major piece of equipment for a term of five years.

Assume: $L = 1,000,000; R = 500,000; k_l = .12; k = .10; n = 60.$

Result:
$$MV = \left(1,000,000 / PVIFA_{(.12/12),60} \right) \left(PVIFA_{(.10/12),60} \right)$$
$$+ 500,000 \left(1 / \left(1 + .10/12 \right)^{60} \right)$$
$$= \left(1,000,000 / 44.955038 \right) \left(47.065369 \right)$$
$$+ 500,000 \left(.6077886 \right)$$
$$= 1,046,943.15 + 303,894.30$$
$$= 1,350,837.45$$

This example is for a commercial lease. Most consumer leases are for automobiles and their terms can vary with respect to the amount to be amortized relative to the original value of the asset. The key to appropriate market valuation of leases is the estimate of average residual value.

Nonaccrual or impaired loans must be valued after close examination of the portfolio. It may be necessary to adjust the contractual cash flows downward to a more reasonable estimate of actual anticipated receipts. It may be necessary to increase the discount rate by some risk premium that is higher than normal. Once these issues have been addressed, the market value of nonaccrual loans is the present value of the adjusted cash flows.

$$MV = \sum_{t=1}^{n} \frac{CF_t}{(1+k)^t}$$

where CF_t = adjusted anticipated cash flow in year t

                      k = normal discount rate plus an additional risk premium

The market value of the *reserve for loan loss* is directly linked to the market value of loans. If credit risk has been incorporated into the discount rate for loan valuation, then the reserve for loan loss is not necessary for valuation purposes.

On the other hand, if credit risk has not been explicitly considered in the discount rate, an estimate of the reserve for loan loss will be required. One objective approach for valuing the reserve is to set it equal to the same percentage of the market value of loans as the book reserve is to the book value of loans. In any event, as long as the assumptions used in valuing the reserve are consistent with assumptions used for valuing the loans themselves, the estimate will be reasonable.

Other Assets

Bank premises and equipment do not lend themselves to a present value analysis because they are not financial assets that yield measurable cash flows. Their market valuation is best estimated by professional appraisals. Other real estate owned is another category of assets that should be valued via up-to-date appraisal.

Investments in subsidiaries can be evaluated using present value analysis. It is necessary to first value the assets and liabilities of the subsidiary at market. In this way, an implied (market value) equity of the subsidiary may be established. The parent bank's asset is then the proportional share of the implied equity of the subsidiary.

Liabilities

The market value of liabilities will be closer to the book value because many are relatively short-term and some are due on demand. The largest divergence of market value from book value will be in long-term borrowings. The major categories of liabilities are:

- Deposits due on demand, including transactions and savings accounts
- Time deposits
- Short-term borrowings
- Long-term borrowings

Transactions accounts are legally due on demand at book value; savings accounts are effectively due on demand at book value because the notification requirement is generally waived. Market value of these liabilities is equivalent to book value.

Time deposits include both small and large time deposits with maturities from seven days to seven years or more. The market value will depend on the face amount of the deposit, the deposit rate, the time to maturity, and the appropriate discount rate.

$$MV = \frac{D\left(1 + \dfrac{k_D}{m}\right)^n}{\left(1 + \dfrac{k}{m}\right)^n}$$

where D = deposit amount

k_D = deposit rate

m = number of times per year interest is paid or compounded

Consider the example of a large two-year CD.

Assume: $D = 1,000,000; k_D = .06; k = .065; m = 4; n = 8.$

Result: $MV = 1,000,000(1.015)^8\left[1/(1.01625)^8\right]$

$= 1,000,000(1.12649259)(.87901347)$

$= 99,202.16$

Notice that even with a 50-basis-point difference
between the deposit rate and the discount rate, the market value of this CD is 99.02 percent of the book value.
This example illustrates that the impact of the time value
of money on short-term liabilities is minimal.

Short-term borrowings include *federal funds purchased
(overnight)*, *term federal funds purchased*, and *securities sold
under agreement to repurchase*. These are liabilities with a
maturity of well under one year. As a result, the difference between book value and market value will be
small. The actual models for valuation are the same as
for the corresponding asset categories (federal funds
sold, term federal funds sold, securities purchased
under agreement to resell).

Another form of short-term borrowing is commercial paper, a short-term liability of a bank-holding company that is usually sold on a discount basis. The original maturity is no more than 270 days (to avoid the necessity to issue a prospectus) and the market valuation model is similar to the model for Treasury bills.

$$MV = M - M(k)\left(\frac{N}{360}\right)$$

where M = maturity value

             N = number of days before maturity

Consider a new 270-day issue.

Given: $M = 1,000,000; k = .045; N = 270.$

Result: $MV = 1,000,000 - 1,000,000(.045)(270/360)$

                $= 1,000,000 - 33,750$

                $= 966,250$

It should be noted that the market rate for the commercial paper can change over the life of the issue. The original discount rate plays no role in market valuation. The value in the secondary market depends on the maturity value, the time to maturity, and the market interest rate only.

Long-term borrowings usually take the form of subordinated notes and debentures. In order for these instruments to qualify as regulatory capital, the instruments must be subordinated to deposits and have an average original maturity of at least seven years. These liabilities are valued using the same models developed for debt securities held as assets. The exact model will depend on whether the bonds are interest-paying or zero-coupon.

Embedded Options

An *option* is an agreement that confers the right to buy or sell an asset or stream of cash flows at a set price through some future date. A *call option* confers the right to acquire an asset or cash flow stream at the exercise price through the expiration date while a *put option* confers the right to dispose of an asset or cash flow stream at the exercise price through the expiration date. Commercial bank portfolios contain options that are not separately disclosed. These options are contained in the securities and loan portfolios:

- Callable bonds
- Mortgages and mortgage-backed securities
- Variable-rate loans with interest rate caps and floors

When the bank owns the option, it has a *long position*, that is, the option is an asset. If the underlying instrument is also an asset for the bank, the long option position adds to the market value of the asset. If the underlying instrument is a liability for the bank, the long option position reduces the market value of the liability.

When another party owns the option, the bank has a *short position*, that is, the option is a liability. If the underlying instrument is an asset for the bank, the short option position reduces the market value of the asset. If on the other hand, the underlying instrument is a liability, the short option position increases the market value of the liability.

These concepts may be summarized as follows:

Bank's Option Position	Effect on Market Value	
	Assets	Liabilities
Long	Increase	Decrease
Short	Decrease	Increase

In the case of *callable bonds*, the call provision of a bond reduces the bond's market value in the bank's investment portfolio. The relationship between callable bonds and noncallable bonds is:

$$MV_N = MV_C + C$$

where MV_N = market value of a noncallable bond

MV_C = market value of a callable bond

C = market value of a call option

Put another way, a commercial bank that owns a callable bond has a long position in a noncallable bond and a short position in the call option.

$$MV_C = MV_N - C$$

The call price stipulated in the bond indenture is the exercise price of the call option. Appropriate valuation for this embedded option is discussed in Chapter 6 in the section entitled "Interest Rate Derivatives."

In order to evaluate the option embedded in *mortgages* and *mortgage-backed securities*, it is necessary to make an assumption about prepayments and then determine the net affect of these prepayments under various interest rate scenarios. The steps in the process are:

- Determine the cash flows of the portfolio under the assumption of *no prepayments.*
- Determine the cash flows of the portfolio *with prepayments.*
- Determine the value of the portfolio under both assumptions with one interest rate environment.
- Determine the difference between the market value of the portfolio with no prepayments and the market value under the prepayment assumption.
- Change the interest rate assumptions as many times as desired, revalue the portfolio with and without prepayments, and compute the difference in present value in each case.
- Estimate the probability of each interest rate scenario.
- Weight the present value differences by their respective probabilities to arrive at the value of the option.

Variable-rate loans have a market value that is close to book value because when required market rate changes, the loan (coupon) rate also changes. If the extent to which the loan rate can float is restricted, the virtual equality between book and market values will not be sustained in all interest rate scenarios. In the case of *variable rate loans with interest rate caps and floors,* these embedded options have not been explicitly priced.

If a loan has an *interest-rate cap,* the borrower has the effective right to receive from the bank the stream of cash flows representing interest payments above the cap rate. These cash flows exactly offset the higher interest payments that the borrower would otherwise be required to make. In other words, the borrower can call or buy a cash flow stream from the bank that is equivalent to the interest payments above the cap level, exactly offset the obligation to pay the bank interest payment above the cap level, and have net zero cash outflows above the cap level. The borrower owns a call option for which there is no exercise price. The call is automatically exercised when interest rates increase. From the bank's perspective, an interest rate cap is a short position in a call option. This short position reduces the value of the loan.

$$MV = L - V_C$$

where L = book value of loan

           V_C = value of the embedded call option

On the other hand, an *interest rate floor* is the minimum interest rate that a variable-rate loan must pay. When a floor is associated with a variable-rate loan, the bank has the right to receive from the borrower the cash flows to replace the amounts not earned because of declining interest rates. In other words, the bank can put or sell an obligation to pay interest payments below the floor (forgone interest payments), reinstate the obligation to pay a higher rate, and receive the cash flows. In this case, the bank owns a put option. There is no exercise price and the option is automatically exercised when interest rates decline. A floor is a long position in a put option. The value of this put option increases the value of the loan.

$$MV = L + V_P$$

where V_P = value of embedded put option

The valuation of caps and floors is discussed below in Chapter 6 in the section entitled "Interest Rate Derivatives."

Exhibit 5-8 summarizes the impact of embedded options on the value of the assets with which they are associated. As a result these effects, assets with embedded options should not be grouped with other assets for valuation purposes.

Exhibit 5–8

Embedded Options and Their Effect on Bank Portfolios

Underlying Instruments	Option	Position	Effect
Callable bonds	Call	Short	Reduces value of bonds
Mortgages and mortgaged-backed securities	Call	Short	Reduces value of assets
Variable-rate loans:			
Caps	Call	Short	Reduces value of loans
Floors	Put	Long	Increases value of loans

Summary

These concepts form a consistent approach to the valuation of a bank balance sheet. They permit an objective assessment of the value of the bank that is not simply based on some multiple of book value.

Selected References

Baughn, William H., Thomas I. Storrs, and Charles E. Walker. *The Bankers' Handbook*, 3e, Homewood, Illinois: Dow Jones Irwin, 1988.

Fabozzi, Frank J. *Fixed Income Mathematics*, Chicago: Probus Publishing Company, 1988.

Federal Deposit Insurance Corporation. *Statistics on Banking 1993*, Washington, D.C.: Author, 1994.

Fitch, Thomas. *Dictionary of Banking Terms*, Hauppauge, NY: Barron's Educational Series, Inc., 1990.

Gibson, Rajna. *Option Valuation: Analyzing and Pricing Standardized Option Contracts*, New York: McGraw-Hill, Inc., 1991.

Howe, Donna M. *A Guide to Managing Interest-Rate Risk*, New York: New York Institute of Finance, 1992.

Hull, John. *Options, Futures, and Other Derivative Securities*, Englewood Cliffs, New Jersey: Prentice Hall, Inc., 1989.

Maroney, Richard F., Jr. "Independent Stock Appraisals Can Pay Off for Small Banks," *Bank Management*, August 1993, pp. 12-16.

McCoy, John B., Larry A. Frieder, and Robert B. Hedges, Jr. *BottomLine Banking: Meeting the Challenges for Survival & Success*, Chicago: Probus Publishing Company, 1994.

Endnotes

1   For example, FASB has indicated the use of DCF in connection with required market value disclosures (SFAS #107) and measurement of loan impairment (SFAS #114).

2   See Appendix A for a summary of time value of money concepts.

3   Mortgage pass-through securities are subject to a *servicing fee* charged by a third party to cover the cost of collecting monthly payments, record-keeping, and sending periodic statements to mortgage borrowers. The coupon rate on the mortgage does not change. Instead, the owner of the pass-through receives less interest. For example, if a mortgage pool pays 8 percent and the servicing fee is .5 percent, the pass-through investor receives interest of 7.5 percent. As the balance declines, the net interest to investor and the servicing fee also declines. This process is illustrated in the section entitled "Embedded options."

4   Alternatively, the payments in the early years may be computed based on lower interest rates. In such a case, PR^t is the difference between the normal payment and the computed lower payment.

5   See Appendix A for time value of money concepts.

6

Valuation Techniques, Part II: Off-Balance Sheet Categories and Fee Income

Introduction

Off-balance sheet items cover a wide spectrum of activities. Some are extensions of traditional lending services and investments, while others are derivative securities that are exchange-traded instruments. The basic categories are:

- Unused commitments
- Letters of credit
- Loans transferred with recourse
- When-issued securities
- Interest rate derivatives

Valuing Off-Balance Sheet Items

Unused Commitments

A *loan commitment* is a lender's agreement to make a loan at a quoted rate for a specified period of time. The loan commitment may be documented in a commitment letter from the bank indicating willingness to lend to a borrower under specified conditions. This letter is a common notice when lending is secured by real estate, including home equity lines of credit and second mortgages. In the commitment letter, the borrower may be protected against interest rate increases via a lock-in period, usually 30 to 60 days. However, the commitment letter also will often specify that the offer to lend may be rescinded in the event of adverse changes in the borrower's financial condition.

To the extent that these loan commitments are outstanding but not yet funded, these unused commitments represent a liability for the bank. The correct valuation of these off-balance sheet liabilities is to find their expected value, that is, the sum of the individual commitments multiplied by their probabilities of being funded.

$$MV = \sum_{i=1}^{n} p_i UC_i$$

where p_i = probability that the loan commitment to client i will be funded

UC_i = amount of the unused loan commitment to client i

Probabilities that the loan commitment will be funded must be subjectively determined based on past experience, current interest rate environment, and specific financial circumstances of the bank client.

Letters of Credit

A *letter of credit (L/C)* is slightly different from a loan commitment in that the L/C usually guarantees payment to a third party on behalf of the bank's client. Essentially, a letter of credit substitutes the credit of the issuing bank for the credit of the client. For example, an importer or exporter is authorized to write drafts up to a specified amount that are payable by the issuing bank.[1] L/Cs are widely used in banking in connection with trade financing.

The extent of the bank's commitment with respect to letters of credit is determined by several factors.

- An *irrevocable L/C* cannot be canceled before a specified date without agreement by all parties involved. On the other hand, a revocable L/C may be amended at any time by the issuing bank.
- A *confirmed L/C* has been endorsed, guaranteeing all payment of all drafts written against it, while an unconfirmed L/C does not carry these guarantees.
- A *standby L/C* is contingent on the bank client's failure to perform under terms of a contract, such as the client's issuance of commercial paper.

The valuation of these off-balance sheet liabilities of the bank should be determined by the same approach noted above for unused loan commitments. However, the probabilities used will differ depending upon the L/C involved. For example, a ranking of these L/Cs in descending order of probability of being funded by the bank may be:

- Confirmed L/C
- Unconfirmed irrevocable L/C
- Unconfirmed revocable L/C
- Standby L/C

The appropriate specific probabilities will depend on the bank's past experience and current circumstances surrounding the underlying transactions.

Loans Transferred With Recourse

Bank loans may be sold to third parties either (1) *without recourse*, implying no further obligation if the original borrower prepays or defaults, or (2) *with recourse*, giving the purchaser of the loans the right to receive payment from the seller of the loans (bank) for failure of the original borrower(s) to pay when due or for prepayments. If the loans are sold without recourse, the bank has no further liability. However, if the loans are sold with recourse, the bank has a contingent or off-balance sheet liability.[2]

Statement of Financial Accounting Standards #77 stipulates that certain items must recorded by the seller of the loans at the date of sale:

- Probable adjustments for probable credit losses, effects of prepayments, and defects in the

eligibility of the transferred loans (to be
recorded as a liability).
- As applicable, a deferral of that portion of the
sales price that represents servicing fees for
future periods (to be recorded as a liability).
- As applicable, an intangible asset representing
excess prepaid servicing fees.

Under generally accepted accounting principles
(GAAP), after the date of sale, the recourse liability related to probable adjustments will be charged with any
actual losses incurred and an expense for the period
recorded. In the case of the unearned servicing fees, an
appropriate amount of income will be recorded for normal servicing fees, reducing the liability.

It should be noted that under regulatory accounting
principles (RAP), a sale of loans may be considered a
borrowing and the assets remain on the books with a
corresponding liability for the cash proceeds. Any of the
following will necessitate this treatment under RAP:

- A put option owned by the purchaser of the
loans allowing the resale to the bank.
- Sale that is secured by a credit arrangement
issued by the selling bank or by a third party
with risk falling back to the selling bank.
- Sale that is secured by an insurance contract in
which the selling bank indemnifies the insurance company against loss.
- Sale of a short-term loan that is part of a long-
term credit commitment by the bank (a "strip
participation").

However, the above-mentioned RAP treatment does not apply to a sale of mortgage loans to Government National Mortgage Association (Ginnie Mae), Federal National Mortgage Association (Fannie Mae), or Federal Home Loan Mortgage Corporation (Freddie Mac).

In valuing loans transferred with recourse, the critical question is whether the existing liability that has been established for probable adjustments is:

- Reasonably stated (no adjustment necessary)
- Excessive (market value is lower than book value) or
- Deficient (market value is greater than book value)

Two primary factors that should be considered are past experience (with respect to default) and the current interest rate environment (with respect to prepayments).

When-Issued Securities

The *when-issued securities* market involves the conditional trading in government bonds or other securities in the interval between the announcement date and the date of actual issue, that is, before the effective listing date. In the case of U.S. Treasury securities, this trading begins immediately after the formal announcement of new bills, notes, and bonds. Initially, when-issued trading is done on a discount basis for bills and on a coupon (yield) basis for notes and bonds. Once the auction results for notes or bonds have been announced, however, when-issued trading in these securities is done on a price basis. Settlement dates are the settlement dates for the respective auctions.

When-issued securities must be valued on the basis of their:

- Commitments to purchase and
- Commitments to sell

In the case of a commitment to purchase, the net value of the transaction is the market value of the when-issued security less the purchase price.

$$MV = MV_{WI} - PP$$

where MV_{WI} = market value of the when-issued security

     PP = purchase price

In the case of a commitment to sell, the net value of the transaction is the sale price of the when-issued security less its market value.

$$MV = SP - MV_{WI}$$

where SP = sale price

Interest Rate Derivatives

An *interest rate derivative* is a contract that involves an interest-sensitive product or the exchange of interest rates on a specified underlying position. Some are negotiated between two counterparties, while others are exchange-traded contracts. The major classifications for interest rate derivatives are:

- Swaps
- Futures and forwards
- Options
- Caps, floors, and collars

Swaps. An *interest rate swap contract* is an agreement
between two counterparties to exchange interest payments for a specified period of time at predetermined
intervals. Swap contracts do not involve purchasing
financial market instruments. Instead, the rights to
future cash flows are exchanged. Alternatively, the
obligations to pay future cash may be exchanged. The
fundamental concept is to exchange a fixed rate cash
flow stream with a floating rate stream.

The most basic interest rate swap is a *coupon swap*
in which a floating rate is exchanged for a fixed rate.
For example, a financial institution may hold a large
portfolio of fixed rate loans while most of its deposit
liabilities are floating rate CDs. Another bank may hold
considerable variable rate investments with fixed rate
obligations. To minimize interest rate risk, the two
institutions may agree to swap interest payments on
liabilities.

The two banks agree upon a *notional principal*, or the
amount of liabilities for which interest rates will be
swapped. Note that this notional amount does not change
hands but is simply the basis for interest rate calculations.
The swap agreement also establishes the maturity date of
the swap and the frequency of payments. When the swap
arrangement involves exchanges of interest rates on
assets, it is called an *asset swap*. When the exchange is on
liabilities, it is a *liability swap*. For example, Bank C (with
fixed rate liabilities) may enter a liability swap that stipulates a $50 million notional amount for four years with
payments made semiannually.

If its fixed rate on liabilities is 4%, Bank C may agree
to swap the fixed 4% for a floating rate of "Treasury bill

plus 1.5," meaning 1.5 percentage points or 150 basis points above the Treasury bill rate.[3] Bank C:

- Has agreed to pay "T-bill plus 1.5"
- Has agreed to receive 4%
- Is referred to as the *floating-rate payor*
- Is said to have sold a swap and has a short position in the swap market

Of course, Bank C's counterparty:

- Has agreed to pay 4%
- Has agreed to receive "T-bill plus 1.5"
- Is referred to as the *fixed-rate payor*
- Is said to have bought a swap and has a long position in the swap market

The swap agreement does not change the way Bank C pays or records its interest expense on liabilities. Bank C continues to pay its fixed rate obligations on the notional principal as would otherwise be the case every six months (in thousands).

	DR	CR
Interest expense	$1000	
Cash		$1000

The effect of the swap agreement is recorded via a separate entry. If "Treasury bill plus 1.5" is 4.75%, Bank C loses .75% or 75 basis points on an annual basis for the 6-month period because Bank C must pay the 4.75% and receive only 4%. The 75-basis-point difference for six months on $50 million is $187,500 [$50 mil. × .0075 × .5]. When Bank C makes the payment to its counterparty, the following entry is made (in thousands).

	DR	CR
Interest expense	$187.5	
Cash		$187.5

Bank C pays this amount to its counterparty in the swap and its own interest expense is increased.

If "Treasury bill plus 1.5" is 3.95% in the following 6-month period, the first entry is the same (in thousands).

	DR	CR
Interest expense	$1000	
Cash		$1000

But Bank C has saved .05% or 5 basis points, amounting to $12,500 [$50 mil. × .0005 × .5] because Bank C pays 3.95% and receives 4%. Bank C receives this amount from its counterparty and records it in the following entry (in thousands):

	DR	CR
Interest expense	$12.5	
Cash		$12.5

This entry reduces the net interest expense of Bank C to $987,500 ($1 mil.–$.125 mil.).

The value of a swap is the present value of the differential interest payments (a negative $187,500 in the first example and a positive $12,500 in the second example). Each of these payments should be discounted at the appropriate rate that applies to a zero-coupon instrument of the same duration.

The difficulty with this process is that, for the most part, the variable rate payments are not known with certainty at any given time. The exception to this is the next floating rate payment. This payment is known because the interest rate is set at the beginning of the period. However, it is also true that on the next reset date for the floating rate side, the rate that is set for the subsequent period will exactly equal the market rate. That is, the floating rate side will have a market value equal to the notional amount on the next reset date. Thus, instead of projecting future variable payments, it is necessary only to find the present value of the next floating rate payment and the notional amount, using the currently prevailing market rate as the discount rate.

$$V_{FL} = \frac{NA\left(\dfrac{k_{FL'}}{m}\right) + NA}{\left(1 + k_{FL}\right)^t}$$

where
V_{FL} = value of the floating rate side of swap

NA = notional principal

$k_{FL'}$ = Floating rate established at last reset date

k_{FL} = Current level of the swap floating rate

t = Time to next reset date

The market value of the fixed rate portion of the swap presents a different type of challenge. There is no doubt as to the amount of each of these payments, but it is necessary to establish the correct discount rate to be used. The amount of each payment is the notional amount multiplied by the fixed rate specified in the swap contract. This fixed rate (coupon rate) is normally set to the swap yield at the time that the swap is created (trade date) so that the fixed rate side will be valued at par (notional amount). At the trade date, the fixed rate is generally set equal to a Treasury yield of a specified maturity plus a spread. After the trade date, the appropriate swap yield will change when the specified Treasury yield changes.

To price the fixed payments, it is appropriate to consider each payment as a zero-coupon bond and to discount each payment by the zero-coupon rate that is appropriate for the date on which the payment will be received. Technically, the term structure of interest rates is the relationship between yield on zero-coupon Treasury securities and their maturities. A noncallable Treasury security can be considered a package of zero-coupon securities, with the date of each coupon payment being its respective maturity date. If the yields on such a package of zero-coupon securities are not the same as the yields available on an equivalent coupon-paying bond, arbitrage profits are possible.[4] However, the zero-coupon spot rate curve must be constructed, rather than derived from observed stripped Treasury securities (maturity value separated from coupon payments, creating a zero-coupon bond), because:

- The conventional Treasury market is more liquid than the stripped Treasury market.
- Yields in certain maturity segments of the stripped Treasury market are distorted by

investors who find the strips attractive, bidding up the price and driving down the yield.

- Accrued interest on stripped Treasury securities is taxed, creating a tax disadvantage vis-à-vis coupon-paying Treasury. This disadvantage is reflected in the market yield.

Since this yield curve is constructed, it is called the *theoretical spot rate yield curve* or the *theoretical zero-coupon yield curve*.

Thus, the theoretical spot rate curve is constructed using the conventional Treasury yield information. However, it is necessary to adjust the conventional Treasury yield information because the implied yields in the Treasury yield curve are lower than the theoretical zero-coupon rates. It can be shown that a long-term Treasury security that is selling at par will have a value greater than par when each of the coupon payments is discounted at the yield to maturity (YTM) for Treasury securities that mature on the same date that the coupon payment is made. (For example, a coupon payment that is due two years from now will be discounted at the YTM on a 2-year Treasury security.) This is true because the calculation of YTM assumes reinvestment of all interim cash flows at the YTM. In the case of a zero-coupon security, there is no interim cash flow and there is no reinvestment prior to maturity. The theoretical spot rates must be higher to compensate for this difference. It can also be shown that when all cash flows of the Treasury bond (selling at par) are discounted at the theoretical spot rates, the calculated value is also par value.

The *theoretical spot rates* are the rates which cause the present value of each of the payments associated with a

Treasury security to equal the current market price of the security.

$$P_0 = \sum_{t=1}^{n} \frac{CF_t}{(1+s_t)^t}$$

where P_0 = current market price of Treasury
                       security

             CF_t = cash flow in period t

             n = number of periods to maturity

             s_t = theoretical spot rate for period t

Since each calculation depends on the theoretical spot rates of both the current period and the previous periods, it is necessary to derive the earlier spot rates first and progress period-by-period in the derivation of subsequent theoretical spot rates.

Exhibit 6-1
Theoretical Treasury Spot Rates

To Maturity Date	Maturity Years	Periods	Coupon	Price	YTM[1]	Semiannual Theoretical Spot Rate[1]
Aug 95	.5	1	0	96.87	.03165	.03165
Feb 96	1.0	2	4 5/8	97.90625	.03395	.034187095
Aug 96	1.5	3	7 1/2	100.28125	.0353	.03661406
Feb 97	2.0	4	4 3/4	95.46875	.0360	.036163055

1 Rates in decimal form.

Note: Prices and yields to maturity are as of February 1995.

Exhibit 6–1 illustrates the calculation of theoretical spot rates for a 2-year yield curve as of February 1995. Since coupon interest is paid on a semiannual basis, there are four periods in this 2-year time frame.

The first observed Treasury security on the time line is a 6-month T-bill, a zero-coupon instrument, with a yield of 6.33%. Since this is a zero-coupon security, no adjustment is necessary and the semi-annual theoretical spot rate is the same as the observed rate, that is, 3.165%.

The observed Treasury note that matures in one year has a coupon rate of 4.625%, an asked price of 97:29 or 97.90625, and a YTM of 6.79%.[5] The theoretical spot rate for the second semi-annual period is that rate which will cause the present value of the future cash flows to equal the price, given a theoretical spot rate of 3.165% in the first semi-annual period.

$$97.90625 = \frac{2.3125}{1.03165} + \frac{102.3125}{\left(1+s_2\right)^2}$$

$$97.90625 - 2.241554791 = \frac{102.3125}{\left(1+s_2\right)^2}$$

$$95.66469521\left(1+s_2\right)^2 = 102.3125$$

$$s_2 = \left(\frac{102.3125}{95.66469521}\right)^{\frac{1}{2}} - 1$$

$$= .034187095$$

$$100.28125 = \frac{3.75}{1.03165} + \frac{3.75}{\left(1.034187095\right)^2} + \frac{103.75}{\left(1+s_3\right)^3}$$

$$s_3 = .03661406$$

SIMILARLY

$$95.46875 = \frac{2.375}{1.03165} + \frac{2.375}{(1.034187095)^2} + \frac{2.375}{(1.034187095)^3} + \frac{102.375}{(1+s_4)^4}$$

$$s_4 = .036163055$$

The theoretical spot rates for periods 3 and 4 are calculated using the specific prices and coupon rates associated with observed Treasury securities with 1.5 years to maturity and 2 years to maturity.

Exhibit 6–2
Treasury Bond Valuation Using Theoretical Spot Rates

Periods	Semiannual YTM[1]	Semiannual Coupon	Spot Rate	PVIF	Present Value Using Spot
1	.03165	2.375	.03165	.969320991	2.302137354
2	.03395	2.375	.034187095	.934978818	2.220574693
3	.0353	2.375	.03661406	.897736152	2.132123361
4	.0360	102.375	.036163055	.867536163	88.814014690

Price based on theoretical spot rates	95.468850098
Actual market price	95.46875
Difference	.000100098

1   Rates in decimal form.

In general, the formula to find the theoretical spot rates is:

$$s_n = \left(\frac{(M+I)}{\left(P_0 - \sum_{t=1}^{n-1} \frac{I}{(1+s_t)^t} \right)} \right)^{\frac{1}{n}} - 1$$

Exhibit 6–2 verifies these results. When the coupon payments and maturity of the 2-year Treasury note are discounted using the theoretical spot rates, the sum of their present values is 95.468850098 versus the actual observed market price of 95.46875, a difference of only .0001.

These theoretical spot rates then form the basis for determining the present value of the fixed interest payments associated with a swap. For example, if the fixed rate at trade date was "Treasury plus 1," meaning the relevant Treasury rate plus 100 basis points on an annual basis, then 50 basis points should be added to each of the semiannual theoretical spot rates derived above.

The value of the fixed rate side of the swap will be the sum of all future fixed payments discounted at the appropriate rate of theoretical spot rate plus spread.

$$V_{FX} = \sum_{t=1}^{n} \frac{CF_t}{\left(1+(s_t+\alpha)^t\right)}$$

where V_{FX} = value of fixed rate side of swap

              s_t = theoretical spot rate for period t based on Treasury rates

              α = spread over Treasury rate

The value of the swap will be the difference between the value of the floating rate side and the value of the fixed rate side. For the floating-rate payor, the value of the swap is the difference between the value of the fixed rate side (cash flows being received) and the floating rate side (cash flows being paid).

$$MV = V_{FX} - V_{FL}$$

For the fixed-rate payor, the value of the swap is the difference between the value of the floating rate side and (cash flows being received) and the fixed rate side (cash flows being paid).

$$MV = V_{FL} - V_{FX}$$

Futures and Forwards. An *interest rate futures contract* is a publicly traded agreement to exchange a standard quantity of a fixed-income security at a specified date in the future at a predetermined price. An *interest rate forward contract* is similar to a futures except that the agreement is not exchange-traded and the quantity of the underlying asset is not standardized.

The following list includes the most common interest rate futures contracts traded in the United States on the Chicago Board of Trade (CBT), MidAmerica Commodity Exchange (MCE), Financial Instrument Exchange (FINEX, a division of the New York Cotton Exchange), and the International Monetary Market at Chicago Mercantile Exchange (IMM).

Instrument	Denomination	Exchange
Treasury bonds	$100,000	CBT
Treasury bonds	$50,000	MCE
Zero-coupon		
Treasury bonds	$100,000	CBT
10-yr. Treasury notes	$100,000	CBT
5-yr. Treasury notes	$100,000	CBT
5-yr. Treasury notes	$250,000	FINEX
2-yr. Treasury notes	$200,000	CBT
2-yr. Treasury notes	$500,000	FINEX
90-day Treasury bills	$1 million	IMM
90-day Treasury bills	$500,000	MCE
30-day Federal funds	$5 million	CBT
1-month LIBOR	$3 million	IMM
Mortgage-backed bonds	$100,000	CBT
Municipal bond index	$1,000 times Bond Buyer MBI	CBT

Treasury bond and Treasury bill futures have historically been the most actively traded.

The buyer of a futures contract is entitled to purchase the underlying asset at a future date at a specified price. In the interim, if the value of the underlying asset increases, the value of the futures contract also increases. If the purchaser chose to sell the contract instead of taking delivery of the underlying asset, that purchaser would realize a profit.

An institution (or individual) may also enter the market and sell a futures contract which obligates the seller to sell the underlying instruments at some specified date and price. In the interim, if the value of the underlying

Exhibit 6–3
Interest Rate Futures Pricing

Scenario I Cash Flows

	Time Zero	Futures Expiration Date
Buy futures contract:		
No cash flow at time 0	0	
Pay contract price at expiration		$-F$
Pay accrued interest on bond		$-100(k_C)(t)$
Sell bond short:		
Receive price of bond	P_0	
Lend proceeds of short sale	$-P_0$	
Deliver bond (from futures) to cover short		0
Receive proceeds from lending:		
Principal		P_0
Interest		$P_0(k_L)(t)$
Net cash flow:	0	$-F -100(k_c)(t)$ $+ P_0 + P_0(k_L)(t)$

Scenario II Cash Flows

	Time Zero	Futures Expiration Date
Sell futures contract:		
No cash flow at time 0	0	
Receive contract price at expiration		F
Receive accrued interest on bond		$100(k_C)(t)$
Buy bond:		
Borrow price of bond	P_0	
Purchase bond	$-P_0$	
Deliver bond to cover futures		0
Repay borrowing:		
Principal		$-P_0$
Interest		$-P_0(k_B)(t)$
Net cash flow:	0	$F + 100(k_C)(t)$ $-P_0 - P_0(k_B)(t)$

Exhibit 6–3
Interest Rate Futures Pricing (cont.)

Given: k_C = coupon rate of underlying bond with a face value of 100

k_L = lending interest rate, for example, the Treasury bill rate

k_B = borrowing interest rate, for example, the Federal funds rate

$k_B > k_L$

t = time to futures contract expiration

F = futures price

P_0 = current price of underlying bond

Note: It is assumed that time zero is immediately after bond coupon payment.

---

asset decreases, the value of the futures contract also declines. If the seller purchased an offsetting contract (at the now lower price) instead of delivering the underlying asset, that party would again realize a profit.

These are the basic principles that make the use of futures a viable method of hedging against portfolio loss. For example, a securities portfolio manager for a bank may be concerned that the value of the bank's portfolio of Treasury bonds will decline if rates increase. The holdings of Treasury bonds are in the "cash" market— the market of actual transactions in stocks and bonds. The appropriate hedge would be to take the opposite position in the "hedge" market, in this case, the futures markets. Since the bank holds Treasury bonds, it is said to have a "long position" (asset) in bonds in the cash market. Accordingly, the bank portfolio manager would take a "short position" in the futures market by selling Treasury bond futures contracts (liability) for subsequent delivery.

Should rates increase, the long portfolio of Treasury bonds in the cash market will decline in value. However, the futures position can be closed by buying an offsetting contract (settling the liability) at a now lower price. The profit in the futures market will work to offset the loss in the cash market.

The valuation of futures contracts is based on the premise that prices in the futures market and the cash market for a particular interest rate instrument will not provide an opportunity for arbitrage profits. The two scenarios in Exhibit 6–3 illustrate the minimum and maximum prices for interest rate futures contracts, with the following assumptions:

k_C = coupon rate of underlying bond, with a face value of 100[6]

k_L = lending interest rate, for example, the Treasury bill rate

k_B = borrowing interest rate, for example, the Federal funds rate

$k_B > k_L$

t = time to futures contract expiration

F = futures price

P_0 = current price of underlying bond

Both scenarios assume that time zero (today) is immediately after a bond coupon payment, ignore transactions costs, and initial and variation margins on the futures contracts.

Scenario I involves a long position in the futures market and a short position in the bond market. At time zero, a bond futures contract is purchased, requiring no cash outflow. At the same time, in the cash market, the proceeds of a short sale of the bond are lent in money markets at the rate k_L. When the futures contract expires, the futures price and accrued interest on the underlying bond are paid. The bond that is delivered in the futures market is used in the cash market to cover the short position. Also in the cash market, the short-term investment including interest is received. The net cash flow represents the profit in this transaction. To eliminate the possibility of arbitrage profits, this profit must be zero.

$$0 = -F - 100(k_C)(t) + P_0 + P_0(k_L)(t)$$
$$F = P_0 + P_0(k_L)(t) - 100(k_C)(t)$$
$$F = P_0\left[1 + (k_L)(t)\right] - 100(k_C)(t)$$

Thus, the price of an interest rate futures contract is bounded on the lower end by the relationship between the bond price, the bond coupon rate, and the lending rate.

Scenario II involves a short position in the futures market and a long position in the bond market. At time zero, a bond futures contract is sold, resulting in no cash inflow. At the same time, in the cash market, a bond is purchased with borrowed funds, at the interest rate of k_B. When the futures contract expires, the bond that was purchased in the cash market is delivered to the futures market and the futures price plus accrued interest are received. Also in the cash market, the short-term loan including interest is paid. The net cash flow also represents the profit in this transaction. Again, to eliminate the possibility of arbitrage profits, this profit must be zero.

$$0 = F + 100(k_C)(t) - P_0 - P_0(k_B)(t)$$

$$-F = -P_0 - P_0(k_B)(t) + 100(k_C)(t)$$

$$F = P_0\left[1 + (k_B)(t)\right] - 100(k_C)(t)$$

The price of an interest rate futures contract is bounded on the upper end by the relationship between the bond price, the bond coupon rate, and the borrowing rate.[7]

The value of *interest rate forward contracts* can be approximated by the valuation formulas for futures contracts. The differences between the two contracts are related primarily to the markets in which they are offered:

- Futures contracts are standardized, traded on organized exchanges, and have a liquid secondary market. Forwards are not standardized in denomination, are not traded, and have virtually no secondary market.
- Over 90% of futures contracts are not settled by delivery but, instead, by offsetting futures contracts. Forward contracts are settled by delivery.
- Futures contracts are marked to market (variation margins), while forward contracts are not.
- There is credit risk for counterparties in forward contracts, but almost none with futures

contracts because the exchanges on which futures are traded assume credit risk.

Beyond these differences, the futures and forward contracts are similar in construction and the same arbitrage logic is appropriate for both.

Options. As noted earlier in this chapter, an *interest rate option contract* is an agreement that confers the right to buy (call) or the right to sell (put) a standard quantity of a fixed-income security at a set price through some future date. This right is exercisable at the discretion of the option buyer. Characteristics and terminology that are relevant for options include the following:

- *Call* option—confers the right to buy the underlying instrument.
- *Put* option—confers the right to sell the underlying instrument.
- *Exercise* or *strike price*—the price at which the option owner has right to either purchase or sell the underlying instrument.
- *Expiration date*—date through which option owner may exercise the option.

The majority of interest rate options are traded on the same exchanges on which futures contracts are traded.

There are several differing features of options contracts vis-à-vis futures contracts. A futures contract purchaser (seller) must accept delivery of (deliver) the underlying asset or sell (purchase) an offsetting contract to close the position. The purchaser of a call or put option may allow the option to expire without taking any action at all. After an option is purchased, the buyer has *no obligation* to do anything further. This is in contrast to a futures contract in which some later action must be taken to close the contract.

The prices of options are paid in full at the time of purchase, in contrast to the margin deposit that is associated with futures transactions. Option prices are quoted in full points (percentage of face value) plus fractional points (64ths). For example, a quotation of 2–42 on a Treasury note contract ($100,000 face value) means 2 and 42/64 percentage of face value, or $2,656.25. Often, option prices are lower than the required initial margin for a futures contract. Thus, a bank may put in place an options hedge for considerably less expense than a futures hedge. In addition, maximum loss is limited to the price of the option.

As long as the bank purchases the option, the maximum loss is limited to the price of the option. Selling, or writing, an option exposes the writer, in some cases, to unlimited risk. Bank portfolio options hedges are best constructed through options purchases. A long position is assumed by purchasing a call option. A short position is assumed by purchasing a put option. Otherwise, the construction of an interest rate hedge using options on interest rate futures is equivalent to that of a hedge using the futures contracts themselves.

The value of an interest rate option is influenced by a number of factors:

- Market value of the underlying asset
- Exercise price
- Interest rates
- Volatility of the price of the underlying asset
- Time to maturity

The *market value of an underlying asset* will affect a call option and a put option in opposite ways. The higher the price, the more likely a call option will be in-the-money. Since the owner receives the difference between the market value and the exercise price, a higher price will cause that difference to increase and, therefore, the value of the call option to increase. The owner of a put option receives the difference between the exercise price and the market value. The lower the price, the more likely the put option will be in-the-money and the more valuable the put option.

The *exercise price* of a call has a negative relationship to the value of a call option. A higher exercise price reduces the profits for a call owner. For a put option, a higher exercise price increases the profits for a put owner and thus has a positive relationship to put value.

When the *interest rate* increases, the value of a call also increases because the present value of the exercise price (cash outflow) declines. Since the put owner receives the exercise price, higher interest rates reduce the present value of future cash flows. Higher interest rates increase the value of a call option and decrease the value of a put option.

Greater *volatility of the price of the underlying asset* increases the value of a call option and a put option. Volatility is measured as the standard deviation of the rate of return of the underlying asset. The greater the volatility, the more likely that the option will be in-the-money because the price is more likely to increase (in the case of a call option) or decrease (in the case of a put option). Consider an underlying asset whose price never changes, i.e., has a zero volatility. If the call option exer-

cise price is above the current market value or the put
exercise price is below the current market value, there is
no possibility that either option will ever be in-the-
money. A positive volatility will increase the probability.

Time to maturity increases the value of call and put
options because there is more of an opportunity for the
market value of the underlying to move in an advanta-
geous direction. There is a positive relationship between
time to maturity and option value.

The two primary components of the value of an
option are the *intrinsic value* and the *time value*. The
intrinsic value of a call option is the difference between
the current market value and the exercise price.

$$C = MV - X$$

If this difference is negative, the intrinsic value of the
call is zero because the option will not be exercised
under these circumstances.

The intrinsic value of a put option is the difference
between the exercise price and the current market value
and will never be less than zero.

$$P = X - MV$$

The observed price of an option is almost always in
excess of the intrinsic value because of the possibility
that the price of the underlying asset will move in such
a way as to bring the option in-the-money or more in-
the-money.

The most widely used valuation model in this connection is the *Black-Scholes option pricing model*:

$$C = (MV)N(d_1) - Xe^{-kt}N(d_2)$$

where

C = value of a European call option

MV = current market value of the underlying asset

X = exercise price

k = risk free rate of return

t = time to option expiration

$N(y)$ = the probability that an observation from a normal distribution will be less than or equal to y

= cumulative normal probability distribution

$$d_1 = \frac{\ln\left(\frac{MV}{X}\right) + \left(k + \frac{\sigma^2}{2}\right)(t)}{\sigma\left(t^{.5}\right)}$$

where

σ = volatility of underlying asset

= standard deviation of rate of return of underlying asset

$$d_2 = d_1 - \sigma\left(t^{.5}\right)$$

The intuition of the Black-Scholes model is based on the fact that the owner of a call option receives market value of the underlying asset less the exercise price when a call option is exercised. The first term on the right hand side of the equation is market value, weighted by its probability of occurrence—$N(d_1)$. Notice that this probability depends on:

- The relationship of the current market value to the exercise price
- The current level of interest rates
- Volatility of return
- Time to maturity

These, of course, are the factors that are noted above. The second term on the right hand side is the continuously compounded present value of the exercise price, weighted by its probability of occurrence—$N(d_2)$.[8]
The Black-Scholes model is based on several assumptions:

- The volatility of the underlying asset is constant over the life of the option.
- The risk free interest rate does not change.
- The underlying asset is a nondividend-paying stock.
- The option is a European call option, i.e., it may not be exercised until maturity.

These assumptions will affect the result of the Black-Scholes model when it is used for interest-sensitive, coupon-paying instruments.

With respect to volatility, over the life of a bond the volatility decreases because the market value approaches par value. However, as long as the time to bond maturity is substantially longer than the life of the option, the Black-Scholes result will be reasonable.

The second assumption that interest rates are constant over the life of the option will not cause a material distortion of option value over short periods of time.

The third assumption is that the underlying asset pays no dividends. For either a dividend-paying stock or an interest-paying bond, the model may be adjusted by subtracting the present value of the interim payments from the market value.

The fourth assumption is that the option is European, that is, may not be exercised before expiration. It has been shown that an American option paying interim payments (such as dividends or interest) will not be exercised before option expiration as long as the present value of the exercise price exceeds the present value of the interim payments. This means that the value of the American option on such an instrument has the same value as a European option.

The Black-Scholes model for the value of a put option is as follows:

$$P = Xe^{-kt}N(-d_2) - (MV)N(-d_1)$$

where $N(-y)$ = the probability that an observation from a normal distribution will be less than or equal to $-y$

$$= 1 - N(-y)$$

The intuition of this model is that, upon exercise, the owner of a put receives $X - MV$. The first term on the right hand side of the equation is the present value of the exercise price multiplied by its probability. The second term on the right hand side is the current market value multiplied by its probability of occurrence.

Interest Rate Caps. The model that is often used to value interest rate caps is *Black's Futures Option Pricing Model.*

$$C = e^{-kt}\left[(F)N(d_1) - (X)N(d_2)\right]$$

where C = call option on a futures contract

F = current market value of a futures contract of the underlying asset

t = life of the option

The owner of an option on a futures contract will exercise the option if the market value of the futures contract exceeds the exercise price of the option. Upon exercise, the owner of the option receives $F - X$. The pricing model measures this difference based on the current market value of the futures contract and weights each by its probability. The result is then discounted at the risk free rate.

Similarly, the value of a put option on a futures contract is:

$$P = e^{-kt}\left[(X)N(-d_2) - (F)N(-d_1)\right]$$

The owner of a put option will exercise if the exercise price is higher than the market value and will receive $X - F$. The model measures this difference, weights each by its probability and discounts the result.

These models can assist in the valuation of the off-balance sheet positions of a bank. The goal in each case is to arrive at an objective measurement of value in order to properly assess the overall financial position of the bank.

Exhibit 6–4
Fee Income Checklist

Trust Fees

Service charges on deposit accounts

Non-deposit service fees:

> Safe deposit box rental
> Mortgage banking and service fees
> Fees from sale of other assets
> Fees on factored accounts receivable
> Investment banking income
> Corporate finance and syndication fees
> Other service fees

Bank card income:

> Merchant discount fees
> Annual bank card fees
> Other bank card fees

Other income:

> Brokerage income
> Trading account profits and fees
> Asset management fees
> Foreign exchange income
> Bankers' acceptances and letters of credit
> Insurance commissions and earnings
> All other

Valuing Fee Income

A separate evaluation of fee income helps to assess the contribution of various lines of business. Once balance sheet and off-balance sheet items have been analyzed, fees from services should be examined using comparable analytical techniques. These, of course, involve the application of present value concepts. Fees should be projected for a period of five years and discounted using appropriate rates of return, adjusted for risk. The result should be considered an asset for the bank. A checklist of fee income categories is shown in Exhibit 6–4.

Of course, the noninterest expenses of a bank must also be evaluated. These include such items as salaries, employee benefits, premises, and equipment. An analysis of these expenses will involve a 5-year projection of each category and appropriate discount rates. The result should be considered a liability of the bank. Portions of this liability should then be allocated to the appropriate areas of the bank, for example, commercial lending, retail banking, trust, brokerage, trading, and underwriting.

The Total Picture

This approach to valuation can be helpful in considering a potential merger partner or acquisition target. It not only provides an objective assessment of the value of the institution in total, but it also provides insights into how the bank's value can be maximized in the future.

Selected References

Battley, Nick, editor. *The World's Futures & Options Markets*, Chicago: Probus Publishing Company, 1993.

Cox, John C. and Mark Rubinstein. *Options Markets*, Englewood Cliffs, New Jersey: Prentice Hall, Inc., 1985.

Fabozzi, Frank J. *Bond Markets, Analysis and Strategies*, Englewood Cliffs, New Jersey: Prentice Hall, 1993.

Fitch, Thomas. *Dictionary of Banking Terms*, Hauppauge, NY: Barron's Educational Series, Inc., 1990.

Gibson, Rajna. *Option Valuation: Analyzing and Pricing Standardized Option Contracts*, New York: McGraw-Hill, Inc., 1991.

Howe, Donna M. *A Guide to Managing Interest-Rate Risk*, New York: New York Institute of Finance, 1992.

Hull, John. *Options, Futures, and Other Derivative Securities*, Englewood Cliffs, New Jersey: Prentice Hall, Inc., 1989.

Johnson, Hazel J. *Financial Institutions and Markets: A Global Perspective*, New York: McGraw-Hill, 1993.

Jones, Frank J. and Frank J. Fabozzi. *The International Government Bond Markets: An Overview and Analysis of the World's Leading Public Debt Markets*, Chicago: Probus, 1992.

Konishi, Atsuo and Ravi E. Dattatreya, editors. *The Handbook of Derivative Instruments*, Chicago: Probus, 1991.

Pavel, Christine A. Securitization: *The Analysis and Development of the Loan-Based/Asset-Backed Securities Markets*, Chicago: Probus Publishing, 1989.

Endnotes

1   A draft is a payment order that directs a second party to pay a specified amount to a third party (the payee). Although similar to a bill of exchange, the term "draft" is generally used when the second party is a bank. A check is a sight draft (due when presented). A time draft is due at a future date.

2   The Financial Accounting Standards Board has established certain criteria for this off-balance sheet treatment. In order to be recognized as a sale and removed from the balance sheet, a transfer of assets must meet each of the following conditions:

   •   Transferor (bank as seller) surrenders control of the future cash flows associated with the loans, with no option to repurchase at a later date.

   •   It must be possible to reasonably estimate the obligations of the transferor in the case of sale with recourse.

   •   The transferee (purchaser) may not require the transferor to repurchase the loans, except when the amount of the remaining unpaid loans is quite small (a "clean-up" call).

   If one of the above conditions is not met, the transaction is not a sale, but instead is a secured borrowing. The loans remain on the books of the bank and the cash proceeds of the transfer are recorded as a liability. The discussion in this section assumes that these conditions have been met and that the loans are no longer recorded as assets.

3   A basis point is one hundredth of one percent.

4   Arbitrage is the process of buying a security at a lower price in one market and selling it at a higher price in another market. In efficient markets, market participants will bid up the price in the lower-priced market, eliminating arbitrage profits.

5   The fractional portion of the price for Treasury notes and bonds is expressed in 32nds of a point, such that 1/32 equals .03125.

6   The term "bond" is used to signify any fixed-income instrument that accrues interest on its face value.

7 Notice that this is the upper boundary because $k_B > k_L$.

8 It should be noted that the binomial approach is another alternative to option pricing. In this approach, the price of the underlying asset is assumed to either increase by u% or decrease by d% with some also assumed probabilities over a single period. For each subsequent period in the life of the option, these same percentage changes and probabilities apply. Each iteration produces a value for the call option, including, in some cases, zero when the call is out-of-the-money. The various values of the option are then weighted by their joint probabilities to arrive at an option value. Deficiencies of the model are:

- There are abrupt changes in option value rather than continuous changes.
- Percentage changes in the price of the underlying asset are restricted to only two values.
- Probabilities of these price changes are set arbitrarily.

Furthermore, when time to maturity is divided into an increasing number of subperiods, the binomial result converges to the Black-Scholes result.

Accordingly, the Black-Scholes model is used here rather than a binomial approach.

7

Case Studies in
Bank Mergers
and Acquisitions

Introduction

Insights in the issues surrounding bank mergers and acquisitions can be gained by examining specific cases. These examples range from the acquisitive Nations Bank to the mega merger of Chemical and Manufacturers Hanover.

NationsBank

In 1983, Hugh McColl, Jr. became CEO of North Carolina National Bank (NCNB). He immediately took the first steps on a long march that would create NationsBank, now the third largest bank in the United States. The first acquisitions took him through Florida, (1983), Texas (1988), and South Carolina (1990). The bank has also bought financial firms to expand the scope of operations into mortgage servicing, consumer finance, and options. But the chain of events that would propel the financial institution on this journey began with Addison Reese, the first CEO of NCNB, and continued with Tom Storrs, his successor.

Early Expansion (1960–1973)

Addison Reese began his banking career in Maryland and later served as executive vice president of American Commercial National Bank, one of the predecessor banks of NCNB. When American Commercial merged with its rival, Security National Bank of Greensboro, in 1960, North Carolina National Bank was born. The clear objective was to challenge Wachovia Bank and Trust Company, the preeminent state-chartered bank of North Carolina, based in Winston-Salem. As the CEO of NCNB, Addison Reese helped define the bank's culture. The unifying theme was to "Beat Wachovia!" Reese wanted the bank to be a statewide company and he pursued mergers to accomplish this.

Tom Storrs, who would later succeed Addison Reese, brought the concept of the holding company to NCNB in 1967. NCNB Corporation was formed to own the bank and other businesses that would meet the strategic objectives of the company—in North Carolina and in other states. In 1969, NCNB became the largest one-bank holding company in the Southeast with resources of $1.2 billion. The interests owned by the NCNB Corp included an insurance affiliate and NCNB Properties, which purchased the bank's real estate for $12 million and then leased it back to the institution. This freed capital of the bank that could be used to invest in earning assets. NCNB Mortgage Corporation was formed. NCNB Corp raised funds to finance the mortgage and construction loan portfolios by issuing commercial paper. Then in 1969, NCNB purchased Stephen Finance Co., Inc., adding 65 consumer lending and sales finance offices in the Carolinas and Georgia. Although one-bank holding companies became prevalent in U.S. banking, few institutions used the structure to expand their scope of operation to the extent of NCNB.

The bank's expansion was rapid and had attracted the attention of the entire financial community by 1973. The international operation had expanded from the Bahamas to London, where it became active in the Eurodollar market. By the end of its first year in business in 1969, NCNB Mortgage was servicing about $5 million in primarily residential mortgages. In three years, NCNB Mortgage had expanded into South Carolina through an acquisition of C. Douglas Wilson & Co., and into Georgia through the buyout of Blanchard & Calhoun. The combined mortgage portfolios of NCNB Mortgage and C. Douglas Wilson amounted to more than $625 million. Blanchard & Calhoun also took NCNB into the growing real estate market of Orlando, Florida, with offices there and in Jacksonville.

By the time of these later acquisitions, NCNB Mortgage was no longer involved in simply residential mortgages. The firm was now underwriting construction of office buildings, shopping centers, manufacturing plants, apartments, condominiums, and residential developments. The company also had an interest in resorts in the North Carolina mountains and along the

Atlantic coast, golf courses, and even a theme park in Myrtle Beach called Pirate Land.

When Tom Storrs took over in January 1974, NCNB Corporation included the nation's 26th-largest bank, with $3.6 billion in assets. Although the bank was the core business, nonbank activities included commercial and residential mortgages, consumer finance, and investment counseling offices in six states and two foreign countries. NCNB was the first bank to have entered the credit card business in the Southeast and one of the first six institutions in the country to win approval for an automated bank branch, installed on the Duke University campus in Durham.

The Sobering Recession (1974)

Three-quarters of the bank's asset base was financed with borrowed money. By the spring of 1974, the Federal Reserve was sending signals that monetary expansion was becoming a real concern for monetary policy makers. Market interests were rising, implying pressure on bank profits, especially for those institutions with a heavy reliance on short-term money markets. At NCNB, these problems had to be addressed by Hugh McColl, who was in charge of commercial and international business, as well as raising funds for the bank. McColl had started his tenure with the bank as a management trainee of American Commercial in 1959. He was willing to take risks, a quality that appealed to Addison Reese, NCNB's first CEO. Now the weight of these economic issues fell squarely on his shoulders.

In May 1974, Storrs was the first banker to broach these issues with New York securities analysts in a regularly scheduled briefing on earnings. Earnings would decline for the first time after 41 straight quarters of increases. Before Storrs had completed his address, stock brokers were leaving the room to contact their West Coast offices. "Sell orders" were executed before Storrs had completed his presentation.

The market refused to buy NCNB paper and the bank was forced to turn to lines of credit from Bank of America, Chemical, and Citicorp. In a humbling experience, Storrs and McColl raised a total of $55 million.

The next step was to curtail lending. McColl and a close associate visited every NCNB branch and advised the staff not to extend any new consumer credit or indirect credit, effectively taking the bank out of automobile financing.

But the damage had already been done. Problems surrounded the existing loan portfolios that had been rapidly expanded, especially home mortgages, consumer loans, and loans for mobile homes. A special home mortgage program had been priced at 8%, well below the market level of 10.5%, in anticipation of interest rate reductions. As interest rates moved in the opposite direction, the cost of funds rates moved upward, all profit on these mortgages evaporated, and the bank faced a $55 million investment in the money-losing loans. The easy-credit consumer loan program granted credit on signature only and drained $5.6 million from the bank's reserves. Mobile homes had been financed through TranSouth (the consumer finance subsidiary of NCNB Corp) on a long-term basis, with the funding structured essentially like automobile loans. However, when the state's economy began to feel the impact of

shortened hours and plant closings in the textile and fur-
niture manufacturing industries, 50,000 jobs were lost in
North Carolina, and the unemployment rate doubled to
11%. The bank found itself with a large inventory of
foreclosed mobile homes. There were so many at one
point that it was necessary for the bank to lease space on
small airstrips to park them. This portfolio amounted to
$30 million.

Earnings in 1974 fell to $17.6 million from $26 million
in 1973. Provisions for loan loss totalled $15.7 million,
more than twice the level of 1973 provisions. Interest
expense for the bank was 41% higher in 1973. The holding
company had used lines of credit that averaged $813 mil-
lion per day, up from a $512-million average in 1973.

Seasoned Experience and Interstate Expansion

The watchword within NCNB for several years was
"damage control." In spite of problems in lending and
funding, earnings grew steadily through the late 1970s.
There emerged two different camps within NCNB:

- An ultraconservative group that believed that
  the bank should avoid any possible repetition
  of events of 1974.
- An aggressive group that embraced a corporate culture of competition and pushing the
  limits of the market, that is, following the
  same philosophy that generally had served
  the institution well.

McColl was a member of the latter camp. CEO Storrs
also recognized that stagnation was unacceptable.
However, certain corrective steps were necessary.

- Lending controls were significantly improved.
- By 1978, the percentage of funds raised from the brokers was reduced to 23% (from 75% in 1973).

Nevertheless, any future expansion would be severely limited by a lack of capital.

The future of NCNB would be directly tied to expansion of NCNB's interstate presence—expansion beyond mortgage banking and consumer finance offices in other states. Florida was deposit-rich and there was at least one proponent of the interstate banking in the state. Guy Botts was CEO of Barnett Banks of Jacksonville and had argued the rationale for interstate banking during a speech to the Association of Bank Holding Companies in 1976. In 1978, Botts and Storrs met and discussed the concept at length. The result was that each presented a bill to their respective state legislatures for consideration. There was no interest in either bill on the part of legislators or other commercial bankers.

Not discouraged by the lack of interest in interstate banking, Storrs formed a special NCNB task force in 1980, the Interstate Banking Group, to push the process. The group's charge was to find ways that NCNB could expand across state lines immediately. Possible alternatives identified by the group included:

- Extending installation of automated teller machines in other states.
- Acquisition of savings and loan associations.
- Testing regulatory limits of TranSouth's consumer finance offices.
- Creating industrial banks.[1]

- Opening Edge Act banks.[2]
- Relocating credit card business to other states.
- Founding new state-chartered banks that would be owned in whole or in part by NCNB.
- Increasing the size and activity of out-of-state loan production offices.[3]

The group identified Florida as the most attractive market for NCNB for a number of reasons. Florida:

- Was growing faster than North Carolina.
- Had deposits of $35 billion in 1980 and projected deposits of $60 billion by 1990.[4]
- Seemed to have little competition.
- Appeared to be underbanked. [The state consistently ranked among the highest in population per bank. Branching had only been approved in 1977, but only two branches were permitted within any one year.]

NCNB had purchased a small nondeposit, trust company in Orlando in 1972—the Trust Company of Florida. The company had only $35 million in assets and had been purchased by Addison Reese (first NCNB CEO). Within weeks of this purchase, the Florida legislature had passed a law prohibiting out-of-state ownership of banks. The Trust Company of Florida was grandfathered along with two other trust companies owned by out-of-state institutions.[5] NCNB interpreted the grandfathering provision of the law to permit the three grandfathered institutions to own more than nondeposit trust operations.

If the NCNB interpretation could be upheld, Florida National Bank appeared to be the perfect acquisition target. Florida National had $2.5 billion in assets and a network of 40 banks. However, B.K. Roberts of Tallahassee, a retired state Supreme Court chief justice with longstanding ties to the Florida banking community, suggested to McColl that NCNB look for an easier target— a clean, quick purchase through which the bank could test its interpretation of the law. Roberts advised that NCNB look for:

- A small bank located in a county where NCNB has no office (to avoid antitrust arguments).
- A limited number of shareholders (to facilitate a quick decision).
- An institution that is in need of financial support (to more easily get permission from banking regulators).

Storrs was concerned that the state legislature might draft a bill to stop the acquisition before it could be completed. So he directed the NCNB team to locate the right candidate and complete the deal after the legislature adjourned (the first week in June) and before it reconvened (January of the following year). In June 1981, NCNB purchased First National Bank of Lake City, a small bank with $22 million in deposits, limited growth potential, located one hour's drive west of Jacksonville. The institution was closely held by three Iowa businessmen who owned 81.5% of the stock. Sight unseen, First National was purchased at a premium price of $19 million after two hours of negotiation in Jacksonville—one of the most important acquisitions ever by NCNB.

While NCNB awaited regulatory approval of the Lake City acquisition, negotiations for the real target commenced. An acquisition team of twenty, led by Hugh McColl, was headquartered in a Jacksonville hotel. The most problematic issue was the interest of C.A. Cavendes Sociedad Financiera of Caracas, Venezuela, which had accumulated 33% of Florida National stock and appeared to be launching a takeover attempt of their own. Florida National negotiators told McColl that they would work with NCNB if McColl could take the Venezuelans out of the picture. McColl delivered, getting the Venezuelan investors to agree to stall any takeover efforts. Then, after several weeks of negotiations between NCNB and Florida National officials, the announcement was made on June 22 that NCNB had structured a bid for the large Florida bank in the amount of $210 million.

But Florida National management reacted coolly to the announcement indicating to the press that Florida National had not solicited the bid. The Florida institution later backed out of the negotiations. It seems that Florida National management only wanted NCNB to buy them enough time to negotiate a deal with a "white knight." Chemical Bank of New York purchased an option to buy Florida National at such time as Florida law permitted interstate banking.[6] Thus, the frustrated NCNB team was left with only its Lake City acquisition.

This is not to suggest that the significance of the Florida entry was in any way diminished. In fact, on one occasion during a lighter moment, a smiling McColl and four of his most trusted lieutenants posed for a photograph in camouflage military head gear, staking their claim with a Florida state flag in Iwo Jima posture. Military metaphors have been a recurring theme in the McColl management team. In fact, the most meritorious award that is given each year by McColl to a Nations-Bank employee is a crystal hand grenade.

NCNB received regulatory approval for the Lake City acquisition and there was no court battle from the Florida banking community. Adverse reactions by Florida bankers were tempered by NCNB discussions (1) with the other two banks operating in same county as their acquisition target and (2) with influential bankers in other parts of the state.

Other acquisitions in the state of Florida followed:

- Gulfstream Banks, Inc. of Boca Raton, $787 million in assets, 20 branches in Broward (Fort Lauderdale) and Palm Beach counties.[7]
- Exchange Bancorporation, Inc. of Clearwater/ St. Petersburg, $1.6 billion in assets, 44 branches in 10 Florida countries.[8]
- Ellis Banking Corporation, $1.8 billion in assets, 70 offices along the West coast of Florida.

Through these acquisitions in Florida, NCNB brought interstate banking to the Southeast. Through the bank's lobbying efforts, the dialogue concerning reciprocal interstate agreements between states was promoted in earnest. With the Ellis acquisition, Storr's last official assignment before retirement, the assets of NCNB grew to $11.6 billion.

The Precedent-Setting Acquisition in Texas

Hugh McColl became CEO in 1983. By 1988, he had expanded NCNB into six important Southern states, North Carolina, South Carolina, Florida, Georgia, Maryland, and Virginia—all experiencing faster growth than the national average. The bank's assets grew to $65 billion with the acquisition of First RepublicBank in Texas through a controversial partnership with FDIC.

While NCNB looked toward Texas for possible merger activity, the Southeast banking compact region stopped at the Mississippi River and, thus, did not include Texas. The Texas banking market had fallen on extremely hard times with the collapse of the oil industry. During the first quarter of 1988, the holding company of First RepublicBank reported a net loss of $1.5 billion and a decline in subsidiary bank deposits of $3.6 billion. The FDIC stepped in and guaranteed all deposits, including those over $100,000 and loaned $1 billion to the two largest subsidiary banks.

In 1988, NCNB helped the FDIC rescue First RepublicBank, with $32.5 billion in assets, the largest bank outside of New York, Chicago, and California. Only a few banks were both large enough and healthy enough to take on this challenge. NCNB crafted a transaction that would change the way that FDIC handled similar situations in the future.

At the time, NCNB had only $28 billion in assets and seemed to be an unlikely candidate to rescue $32-billion First RepublicBank. But McColl made a personal appeal to then Chair of FDIC, L. William Seidman, noting NCNB's ability to merge and operate banks efficiently. However, McColl noted that NCNB could not take over the bad loans of First RepublicBank. If FDIC took over the nonperforming loans, NCNB was prepared to invest $200 million in the bank and to commit the necessary management to restore the institution to profitability. FDIC was willing to listen. If a satisfactory arrangement could be agreed upon, FDIC power to override state and regional restrictions could position NCNB in a large regional market to which it could not otherwise have access.

Back in Charlotte, the utmost secrecy prevailed. If the press learned of the bank's interest in entering Texas, public confidence in the bank's paper could once again evaporate as it had in 1974. The plan that was delivered to FDIC included a new structure called a "bridge bank." The bridge bank was formed by the sale of the subsidiary banks to a new bank owned jointly by FDIC and NCNB. The original holding company was left as a shell, holding no assets with original First RepublicBank stockholder claims being rendered worthless. During a 90-day transition period, NCNB would determine the fair market value of all assets and liabilities. Then with a $210 initial investment, NCNB would take control of 20% of the new bank with an option to purchase the remaining 80% in five years.

A special asset division would hold the loans with little prospect of repayment. Virtually all the cost for the special asset pool would be absorbed by FDIC.

- NCNB could place an unlimited amount of loans in the special asset pool in the first year and up to $750 million during the second year.
- NCNB losses were capped at 35 basis points of all loan losses for the first year. All loan loss in excess of this limit would be absorbed by FDIC.

- FDIC was to absorb all costs associated with the special asset pool, including funding, administrative, and legal expense.

The first draft was rejected by FDIC—too much downside exposure, too little upside.

After much negotiation, deliberation, and consideration of other bids, the FDIC accepted the NCNB proposal. By March 1989, the deal began to show a profit. NCNB accelerated its buyout schedule, paying $310 million to FDIC in April 1989 for an additional 29% stake, raising its share to 49%. Then in August 1989, four years ahead of schedule, NCNB completed its purchase of the remaining 51% of NCNB Texas for $800 million.

NCNB Texas capitalized on the increasing problems in other segments of the Texas market through acquisitions:

- National Bankshares Corporation in San Antonio with $1.5 billion in deposits.
- An $8 billion home mortgage servicing company.
- A $3.5 savings and loan in Houston.

NCNB set a precedent in the area of mergers and acquisitions in the case of distressed institutions. This kind of aggressiveness has also been demonstrated in expansion into other regions and areas of financial services.

Continued Acquisitions

The merger of NCNB of Charlotte and C&S/Sovran of Atlanta in 1992 created NationsBank. At the time of the merger, NCNB was the tenth-largest bank in the United States and C&S/Sovran was twelfth. C&S/Sovran was struggling under the weight of nonperforming loans that represented 3.3% of the total in early 1991, up from 1.5% the year before. Negotiated in June 1991, the deal involved an exchange of 137 million shares of C&S/Sovran at the exchange rate of .75 share of NCNB for each C&S/Sovran share, for a total value of $4.6 billion. This acquisition added 1000 branches in Georgia and Virginia. The potential cost savings involved as much as $130 million per year in branch overlap in South Carolina and Florida, as well as savings of $150 million per year in overhead reduction associated with headquarters consolidation.

However, the merger was delayed because of regulatory review. The FDIC drew criticism in connection with the concessions that it granted during the First Republic acquisition. The tax benefits that accrued to NCNB effectively shield more than half of the institution's aggregate earnings. In response to criticism of the arrangement, the Federal Reserve extended the period of public comment to November 1991. The merger was ultimately approved and made final in early 1992. As a result of this acquisition, NationsBank became the 4th largest bank with $110 billion in assets.

In 1993, NationsBank acquired MNC Financial, Inc. of Maryland, with offices in Virginia, and the District of Columbia and assets of $17 billion. This deal was valued at $1.38 billion with 50.1% in NationsBank common stock and 49.9% in cash. With this merger, NationsBank had full-service offices in North Carolina, South Carolina, Maryland, Virginia, Washington, D.C., Florida, Georgia, Tennessee, and Texas. Total assets grew to $155 billion.

NationsBank has also aggressively used mergers and acquisitions to enter other areas of financial services. In late 1992, the acquisition of Chrysler First, Inc. was announced. This non-automotive finance subsidiary of Chrysler Financial Corporation. This acquisition, renamed NationsCredit, increased the consumer finance business of NationsBank by a factor of eight, encompassing consumer and inventory finance. Chrysler First represented an addition of receivables of approximately $4 billion and operates in 175 locations in 32 states to the NationsBanc Financial Services subsidiary total of $500 million and 105 offices. The combined NationsCredit offers a wide range of consumer and business services:

- Home equity loans
- Personal lines of credit
- Retail installment lending
- Unsecured personal loans
- Private label credit cards

With a goal of expanding securities trading, NationsBank purchased Chicago Research and Trading (CRT) in 1993. The $225 million acquisition brought to NationsBank a primary government securities dealer and an experienced trader in options and futures contracts. This acquisition permits the bank to offer its clients a wider array of risk-management products. CRT is one of Chicago's biggest and most respected futures and options traders and is experienced in currency swaps, forward-rate agreements, and interest-rate options. Its trading volume is between 100,000 and 200,000 contracts per day with an aggregate face value of $10 billion.

In a two-day period in February 1995, NationsBank announced the purchase of significant mortgage servicing rights from SourceOne Mortgage Services Corporation and KeyCorp Mortgage Inc. SourceOne sold 25% of its mortgage servicing portfolio—115,000 loans with a book value of $10 billion and a weighted average interest rate of 7.72%. The portfolio is a mixture of Fannie Mae, Freddie Mac, and Ginnie Mae loans.[9] The entire residential mortgage servicing business of KeyCorp Mortgage was purchased—390,00 loans with a book value of about $25 billion and a weighted average interest rate of 7.95%. The portfolio was a mix of government and conventional mortgage loans. These two purchases brought the NationsBanc Mortgage Corporation portfolio to $75 billion. The objective is clearly to capitalize on the economies of scale in mortgage servicing activities and to boost fee income.[10]

NationsBank has used the acquisition strategy to expand both geographically and in area of service. The bank has been aggressive in implementing cost savings within acquired institutions by being the clearly dominant player. In the case of other institutions, this lack of dominance can delay the realization of cost savings. An example of this is the merger of equals between Chemical Bank and Manufacturers Hanover.

Chemical Banking

The 1992 merger of Chemical Banking Corporation and Manufacturers Hanover Corporation was truly a merger of equals. This is perhaps best illustrated by selection of the name and logo of the merged institution. The logo, including typeface and striped-square emblem, is that of Manufacturers Hanover while the name is that of Chemical.

The Challenges

By 1993, the new Chemical had saved over $350 million in operating costs. However, it was slow to divest of many businesses that lacked a strong competitive edge. The process of crafting a mission statement illustrates the problems of reaching agreements in mergers of equals. John McGillicuddy (former chairman and CEO of Manufacturers Hanover and first CEO of the merged Chemical Banking), Walter Shipley (former CEO of the original Chemical and chairman and CEO of the merged Chemical Banking as of January 1994), two vice-chairman, and a consultant spent three days in retreat and emerged with the following mission statement describing the bank they hoped to build:

"The best broad-based financial institution, a leader in our chosen markets."

But the arguments that preceded agreement on this statement centered around distinctly different ideas of corporate culture. How should the two work together? Should it be in the investment-banking sense of "partnership?" Was it better to think of it as "teamwork?" Were the staff members and tellers really ready for the concept of "empowerment?"

The promises to the all constituents were tall orders to fill.

- The shareholders were promised that there would be a reduction of $625 million in expenses and 6,200 in employees. There would also be an improvement in the credit rating to AA (from BBB+) and a cap of $100 million for any revenue fall-off during the merger process.

- The customers would not suffer, whether they were savings account holders in Long Island or cash management clients in London.
- Teamwork among workers of both institutions would prevail.

However, the conflicts that existed covered a wide range of issues. For example:

- The former Manufacturers' management style was very centralized while Chemical's was more decentralized in terms of power and responsibility.
- Manufacturers' accounting system gave each individual unit considerable leeway in determining profitability while Chemical's used a uniform set of accounting standards.
- Manufacturers trading activities in currencies was primarily for customers while Chemical actively trading currencies on its own account.

These and other differences in practice and culture significantly slowed the consolidation process. There were many skeptics and the value of the bank's stock fell throughout much of 1993.

A Communications Model

Despite what appeared early on to be protracted consolidation efforts, the merger provides important insights into the correct approach to communicating a merger to all constituents. In 1991, when the time arrived for the announcement, the news was spread with military precision. At stake were the confidence of the stock market, the morale of bank employees, and the image of the new institution in the eyes of the general public. The head of the public relations (PR) team, John Stephans (then senior vice president for communications at Manufacturers and now head of PR for Chemical), went on "vacation" in early July. Stephans told coworkers that he planned to relax at home for a couple of weeks. Instead, he set up shop in the offices of a local PR firm and secretly planned an all-out communications assault.

On Sunday night, July 14, 1991, the boards of both banks approved the merger. At 7:30 a.m. July 15, Shipley and McGillicuddy signed the merger documents in the office of a New York law firm. But Stephans' plan was already underway. Trucks had been dispatched to both banks' outlying locations in synchronized order. The trucks carried copies of a "Dear Colleague" letter from both Shipley and McGillicuddy. The trucks were dispatched so that they might arrive at exactly 8:30 a.m. For those locations outside New York, a closed-circuit broadcast was planned for later in the day designed to reach every officer of both banks with rank above the level of senior vice president. A Manhattan restaurant was rented that evening for a cocktail party to enable employees of the two institutions to become acquainted with their new colleagues.

At 8:30 a.m., the banks released the news to the Dow Jones News Wire, to communicate with the financial markets. There was a press conference between the two chief executives and key reporters. Later in the day, a session with bank analysts helped the communication process with investors.

The communications clearly indicated the probable impact on employees and service to customers. It was explicitly stated that 6,200 jobs would be eliminated and that 70 branches would be closed. An employee hot-line was established to answer questions and the banks soon began a "Merger Update Bulletin" as well. Also on July 14, without disclosing exact locations, a diagram illustrated that no closed branch would be any further than two blocks from a branch that would remain open. It was made clear that remaining branches would receive service upgrades involving a $3 million investment and the installation of 12 new ATMs. These plans were discussed with then Mayor David Dinkins, who praised both institutions for their concern for the community.

The Final Analysis

By virtually all accounts the merger of equals has been a success.

- Shortly after the merger, Chemical raised $1.6 billion in a new equity issue.
- Tier I capital is 7.9% of risk-weighted assets vs. 5.1% in 1992.
- Earnings have increased from almost nothing in 1991 to $1.6 billion in 1993.
- The credit rating has improved to single-A.
- The placement capabilities of the old Chemical have worked well with the originating capabilities of the old Manufacturers to

place the new Chemical at the top of league
tables in global syndications.

- In the New York area, Chemical is now #1 in
  consumer deposits and #1 in small-business
  and middle-market banking.

Essentially, two banks that were broad-based and
diversified have come together to create a genuine pow-
erhouse in a difficult, but fruitful merger of equals.

BankAmerica Corporation

In terms of capital, BankAmerica is the top-ranking U.S.
bank with $6 billion in Tier I capital. Its almost $200 billion in assets earn it a rank second only to Citicorp. The
San Francisco-based holding company has always
aggressively sought to become a truly national bank.

California Operations

Amadeo Giannini founded the Bank of Italy in 1904. His
philosophy of banking leaned toward providing financing for small merchants and farmers as well as reasonably priced mortgage loans, with attention to the personal aspects of banking. For example, after the earth-
quake of 1906, Giannini retrieved the gold, cash, and
notes from the bank before the resulting fire destroyed
them and promptly opened a makeshift branch on a pier
from which he made loans for reconstruction.

Accomplishing the objective of serving the whole state
of California (and ultimately the entire United States)
meant that the bank had to operate outside of San
Francisco. To circumvent the prohibition against intrastate
branching, Giannini purchased the Bank of America of Los

Angeles with 21 branches. In 1928, Giannini formed a holding company Transamerica Corporation to manage the banks and other enterprises. By 1930, both the Bank of Italy and Bank of America were operating as Bank of America.

A Nationwide Focus

Through acquisitions via the holding company format, Transamerica reached outside California, eventually controlling 41 percent of commercial bank office locations, 39 percent of commercial bank deposits, and 50 percent of commercial bank loans in Arizona, California, Nevada, Oregon, and Washington. This much control of commercial banking interests in one company led the Federal Reserve to bring an antitrust action against Transamerica in 1948. Essentially, the court ruled in favor of Transamerica requiring it to divest of Bank of America, but allowing it to retain the remaining 46 banks and to expand into other states if it elected to do so. It was this case and the apparently sympathetic ruling of the courts that led to the Bank Holding Company Act of 1956. The act was intended to prevent the spread of bank holding companies and the broad-based financial services that they offered.

Neither the court decision nor the Bank Holding Company Act dissuaded the Bank of America from its goal of nationwide banking. Transamerica divested its Bank of America in 1958. In the same year, Bank of America introduced Bankamericard, which would later become Visa in 1977. The bank also dramatically increased its international presence, becoming one of the most active international lenders in the 1950s and 1960s in the United States. In 1968, Bank of America became a subsidiary of BankAmerica Corporation.

Problems At Home and Abroad

When A. W. Clausen became CEO in 1970, the bank embarked on an aggressive plan for international and real estate lending. During his tenure, earnings and assets quadrupled. When Clausen left in 1981 to become head of the World Bank, he was replaced by Samuel Armacost, who inherited a number of problems the most serious of which was large loan losses. The aggressive international lending was done with little strategic focus, poor communication between headquarters and overseas locations, and few credit controls. Overhead costs soared out of control and domestic loans to energy, agriculture, and real estate sectors soured. Earnings slumped, as Bank of America lost its ranking as largest U.S. bank to Citicorp. By 1985, Armacost was forced to layoff employees for the first time in the bank's history. The following year, Armacost himself resigned under fire.

Clausen returned as CEO until 1990 during which time the bank reduced both costs and the troubled domestic loan portfolio. In 1990 under the new CEO, Richard M. Rosenberg, BankAmerica acquired eight troubled thrifts and expanded its presence from three states to seven. The back-office operations were modernized in 20 regional centers. At the same time, the bank retrenched from international markets, closing down or consolidating many of its branches.

In California, the focus of Bank of America has clearly shifted to consumer banking. Branches have adopted aggressive merchandising initiatives, including calling on customers to ask what they needed and giving branch managers and employees performance-related bonuses. With the $4.7-billion acquisition of Security Pacific in 1991, BankAmerica tops the ranks of U.S. banks in terms of capital.

The Vision Revisited: The Continental Acquisition

Under Rosenberg, the vision of BankAmerica is not unlike that of Giannini, that is, nationwide banking. With the announcement of its acquisition of Continental Bank of Chicago in January 1994, BankAmerica asserted its long-standing objective of spanning the country with a full range of services. The $1.9-billion purchase of Continental (in roughly equal proportions of cash and stock) enables BankAmerica to expand its presence in wholesale banking and its relationships with large and medium-sized companies in the midwestern United States. Continental has 2,000 corporate accounts, with subsidiaries involved in trust, asset-management, collection, and foreign activities.

In fact, this presence is considered so important that BankAmerica will move its corporate headquarters to Chicago. The Continental acquisition is expected to generate only modest cost reduction, primarily through (1) consolidation of Continental domestic and foreign offices with those of BankAmerica and (2) the elimination of redundant corporate and administrative expense. To prevent dilution of BankAmerica stock, the bank bought back $500 million of its own shares. Within two years of the merger, 500 to 800 jobs are to be eliminated, out of a total of 100,600 positions in the two banks.

The acquisition is also noteworthy in terms of the financial structure.

- The amount of BankAmerica stock issued in the merger was subject to adjustment if its average price during a 10-day period ending 10 days prior to closing was above $55.84 per share or below $36.16 per share.

This provision of the agreement is a "collar" to establish the parameters of the value of the transaction. The upper limit protected BankAmerica from paying too much. The lower limit protected Continental shareholders from receiving too little.

- Continental granted BankAmerica an option to purchase shares of Continental common stock representing 19.9% of its outstanding common stock at a price of $37.50 per share. The option was exercisable under certain circumstances:
  a. The purchase by a third party of more than 20% of Continental shares OR
  b. Continental's completion of an alternative transaction with a third party at a higher price.
- If Continental entered such an alternative transaction, it was obligated to pay Bank-America the greater of $60 million or 3% of the transaction's value.

These provisions provided protection for Bank-America against a bidding war for Continental. Should a third party have accumulated more than 20% of Continental shares, BankAmerica had the right to purchase approximately 20% of Continental shares at a known price of $37.50. Should a third party complete the transaction, BankAmerica also would recover at least $60 million. These provisions protected BankAmerica from the kind of experience by NCNB in its failed quest for Florida National.[11]

In September 1994, the transaction was concluded, with Continental shareholders receiving, for each Continental share, either .7993 shares of BankAmerica stock or $38.2970 in cash. Of the total 49.7 million Continental shareholders, 27.9 elected to receive stock and 21.9 chose cash. Since BankAmerica issued only 21.5 million shares, randomly selected shareholders received cash instead of stock. The Chicago bank will be renamed Bank of America Illinois.

The acquisitions by BankAmerica have helped position the institution to remain a truly global player. According to CEO Rosenberg, "You need a large bank to operate in a global environment."[12]

Banc One

With its $88 billion in assets and $7.5 billion in Tier I capital, there are few U.S. banking institutions that have a higher ranking (in terms of capital) than Banc One Corporation—BankAmerica, Citicorp, Chemical Banking Corporation, NationsBank, J.P. Morgan & Company, and Chase Manhattan.

In 1929, the two Columbus banks Commercial National and City National Bank of Commerce, merged to form City National Bank and Trust. John H. McCoy was the bank's first president. His son John G. McCoy took over in 1958 and shortly thereafter started to break with tradition. In 1966, the bank introduced the first Visa credit card outside of California (then BankAmericard). McCoy formed First Banc Group in 1967, a holding company of which City National was a subsidiary. Then in 1968, the company bought Farmers Savings and Trust of Mansfield, Ohio. By 1985, the holding company owned a total of 44 Ohio banks.

In a 1977 alliance, First Bank Group was designated as the bank to manage the Cash Management Account (CMA) for Merrill Lynch. This innovation brought together a retail brokerage account, a checking account, and a debit card, representing an aggressive post-Glass-Steagall combination of services.

In 1979, First Banc Group changed its name to Banc One and all bank subsidiaries included Bank One in their names.[13] When the third generation McCoy, John B., took over the reins in 1984, the emergence of multistate regional agreements with respect to bank acquisitions had begun. Banc One expanded into Indiana, Kentucky, Michigan, and Wisconsin. With FDIC guarantees against loss, Banc One purchased the loans of 20 of the branches of MCorp (Texas), paying $34 million for $11 billion in assets ($2.5 billion of which were troubled). In 1991, Illinois was added to the list of states in which Banc One operates.

Early on, Banc One grew by acquiring smaller banks, consolidating back-office operations, and mixing local control with regional marketing power. The company continues to stress retail banking, quickly taking advantage of technological advances such as ATMs and home banking systems. With its technology, Banc One maintains a master file that records which products each customer is likely to buy. Its corporate clientele is the middle market. The bank's overall strategy involves conservative lending, innovative technology, dedicated customer service, and mergers with other banks.

In identifying potential candidates for merger, Banc One follows certain guidelines:

- Never merge with a peer.
- Do not buy a bank more than one-third the size of the existing Banc One organization.
- Leave the existing management in place.
- Allow each bank to make its own decisions in a decentralized fashion.

These decentralized operations are coordinated through a system of common products, technology, and monthly reporting requirements.

As the result of these mergers, Banc One's third quarter 1994 asset base of $88.2 billion is almost three times its 1990 level. In addition to traditional basic commercial banking, Banc One is engaged in:

- Data processing
- Venture capital
- Investment and merchant banking
- Trust operations
- Brokerage
- Investment management
- Equipment leasing
- Mortgage banking
- Consumer finance
- Insurance

Banc One has 75 bank subsidiaries with 1,425 offices in Arizona, California, Colorado, Illinois, Indiana,

Kentucky, Michigan, Ohio, Oklahoma, Texas, Utah, West Virginia, and Wisconsin. The Banc One presence now reaches from the Great Lakes to the Gulf of Mexico.

PNC Corporation

PNC Corporation has $64 billion in assets and $4.3 billion in Tier I capital. The First National Bank of Pittsburgh was one of the first banks chartered in 1863 under the National Bank Act passed in the same year. That bank merged with Second National Bank of Pittsburgh in 1913. By 1921, the institution had also merged with Peoples National Bank (Pittsburgh).

In the 1940s, the bank made strategic acquisitions to establish a strong trust business, acquiring Pittsburgh Trust, Sewickley Valley Trust, and Monongahela Trust. The name of the bank was then changed to Pittsburgh National. In 1965 the bank entered the credit card business and joined the Bankamericard program in 1969. The holding company Pittsburgh National Corporation was formed in 1968 and a series of holding company acquisitions followed:

- Pittsburgh National Discount (commercial paper)
- PINACO (insurance on commercial loans)
- Pittsburgh National Leasing (lease financing)
- Pittsburgh National Life (credit life, health, and accident reinsurance).

These acquisitions enabled the bank to enter non-bank financial activities that were permitted within the scope of bank holding companies.

In 1983 another merger strengthened the institution's position in money management and trust operations. Pittsburgh National combined with Provident National of Philadelphia to become PNC Corporation. Acquisitions followed in other parts of Pennsylvania, Kentucky, Ohio, New Jersey, and Delaware.

It should be noted that PNC has had to absorb significant loan losses in recent years, due primarily to real estate exposure in eastern Pennsylvania. Write-offs in 1990 drove return on assets to an uncharacteristically low 0.2 percent. The bank has also undergone a restructuring of back-office operations to achieve greater efficiencies.

Acquisitions during 1994 and 1995 reveal that the bank continues to pursue lines of business in multiple regions and all aspects of financial services. In June 1994, PNC announced the acquisition of First Eastern Corporation, a $2-billion bank in Northeast Pennsylvania. One month later, PNC announced the acquisition of Indian River Federal Savings Bank of Vero Beach, Florida, a $74-million bank. Shareholders in both transactions received cash payments.

Through offices in Vero Beach and Tampa, PNC Trust provides trust and estate administration, investment management, and custody of securities. The Indian River acquisition fulfills the objective of permitting PNC customers to consolidate their Florida banking relationships.

In June 1994, PNC also announced a definitive agreement to acquire BlackRock Financial Management, a New York-based asset management firm, for $240 million in cash and notes. BlackRock provides fixed-income asset management services to individual and institutional investors, including 24 U.S. mutual funds and more than 70 separately managed portfolios, with $23 billion in assets under management. BlackRock clients include pension funds for General Electric Company and Chrysler Corporation. Together, PNC Bank and BlackRock control $75 billion in discretionary assets under management, making PNC the 6th largest bank money manager in the United States. BlackRock is now a subsidiary of PNC Bank Corporation—PNC Investment Management and Research.

In March 1995, PNC announced a definitive agreement to acquire the Chemical Bank New Jersey. The purchase price approximates $504 million, with PNC having the option of issuing up to $300 million of perpetual preferred stock to Chemical Banking Corporation. Chemical retains its northeastern new Jersey banking operations, focused on the metropolitan New York region. PNC gains the southern and central New Jersey offices, consisting of 84 branches in 15 counties with $1.8 billion in consumer loans, $500 million in middle-market commercial loans, and $2.9 billion in retail core deposits. PNC did not accept any nonperforming loans. These offices are adjacent to PNC's existing operations in eastern Pennsylvania and Delaware.

PNC acquisitions that bolstered the fee-generating activities, such as trust operations, have paid handsome dividends. In 1988, noninterest income was not quite $550 million. By 1992, it was $887 million and the bank was earning .95% on assets. Noninterest income in 1993 was $945 million and return on assets had increased to 1.44%. PNC Securities, which offers mutual funds and related products, is projected to employ 500 to 600 brokers by the end of 1995. The bank also has a significant operations in the area of private placement investment banking. In 1993, investment banking activities $208 million in fees.

PNC appears to have found its niche, a strong and diverse geographic banking presence with a wide scope of services that includes consumer banking, mortgage banking, corporate banking, investment management and trust, mutual funds, and investment banking. Much of this positioning has been accomplished through acquisitions of firms in strategically important markets.

Fleet Financial Group

With its roots firmly planted in New England, Fleet Financial Group is the largest banking organization in that region. The 1991 acquisition of Bank of New England, crafted by Kohlberg Kravis Roberts, established Fleet's dominance over long-established Bank of Boston. The 1995 acquisition of Shawmut National Corporation created an institution with an asset base of $80 billion—the only bank among the U.S. top ten that is headquartered in New England.

Fleet Financial began in 1791 as Providence Bank in the Rhode Island city of the same name. The institution evolved into Fleet National Bank and, later in 1968, a subsidiary of Industrial Bancorp, one of the first bank holding companies permitted by law. The holding company changed its name in 1970 to Industrial National Corporation and expanded its scope of operation through a number of acquisitions:

- Southern Discount, Atlanta-based consumer finance company (1973).
- Mortgage Associates, Inc., Milwaukee-based mortgage banking operation (1974).
- Credico, New Jersey-based consumer lending company (1983).
- Norstar, New York-based bank (1988).

These and other acquisitions increased Fleet's asset base from $4.2 billion in 1980 to $32.5 billion in 1990. But it was the Bank of New England and Shawmut acquisitions that attracted the most attention by the financial world.

Precedent-Setting Acquisition of Bank of New England

In January 1990, the Bank of New England finally fell under the weight of bad real estate loans that represented almost 40% of its loan portfolio and generated a 1990 net loss of approximately $650 million. It was the third-largest failure in U.S. bank history and the FDIC needed to find bidders that had enough financial clout to absorb the $20 billion institution.

As it turned out, there was no lack of interest. More than 10 banks expressed an interest in taking over Bank of New England, among them BankAmerica Corporation (with a strong capital position) and Bank of Boston (also affected by the New England real estate slump). Fleet CEO Terrence Murray was interested, but needed financial backing since the bank had just sustained a $48 million loss (related to nonperforming real estate loans). Kohlberg Kravis Roberts & Co. (KKR) also wanted to bid, but hesitated because of a failed bid in 1989 for MCorp, despite presenting the highest bid. It appeared that the FDIC did not want a leveraged buyout firm to run a bank. Fleet needed KKR's deep pockets; most of its investors are pension funds. KKR needed a bank if it was to win the bid.

Fleet and KKR formed an unlikely partnership that submitted the winning bid. The final Fleet/KKR bid was $625 million, of which $487 million was in cash. The FDIC accepted this bid in April 1991 on the grounds that it was the least costly for the bank insurance fund. In exchange, Fleet and KKR investors gained control of one of the largest retail-banking franchises in New England, with a guarantee that they could return any loss-producing assets to the FDIC within three years.

The specifics of the arrangement between Fleet and KKR are as follows:

- Seventy-five investors purchased $283 million of nonvoting dual-convertible preferred stock in Fleet.
  - The stock is convertible into Fleet common stock after three years at $17.65 per share.
  - Alternatively, the preferred can be converted into a 50% ownership stake in Newco, a company that controls much of the former franchise of Bank of New England.
- The investing group also received warrants to buy 6.5 million shares of Fleet common stock.
- As a result of these positions, KKR investor could end up with 16.5% of Fleet, but are not entitled to a seat on the board.

This financial arrangement tests the limits of the Bank Holding Company Act that restricts ownership of a bank by nonbank institutions. But it illustrates the increasing ingenuity that can be observed in structuring bank mergers and acquisitions.

The Shawmut Acquisition

The February 1995 announcement that Fleet Financial Group would buy Shawmut National Corporation created a potentially $80 billion institution. Shawmut had been on an acquisition spree in an apparent attempt to avoid being taken over by another institution, with six announced acquisitions in 1993 and 1994. But early in 1995, Shawmut CEO Joel Alvord approached Fleet CEO Murray, this time seeking a buyer for Shawmut. Shawmut stock had fallen from the mid-$20s in 1994 to as low as $16.375. Major shareholders, especially Fidelity Investments, were pushing for a sale and Fleet would be a friendly acquirer.

The agreed upon price was a $3.45 billion stock swap, in which Shawmut shareholders will receive .8922 newly issued shares of Fleet for each share of Shawmut stock, implying approximately $30 per share. Since Shawmut stock was selling at $20.625 at the time of the announcement, this represented an almost 50% premium.

However, it appears that significant cost savings will be realized as a result of this combination.

- Costs should decrease by as much as $400 million per year or 14% of combined noninterest expenses.
- A net reduction of 10% of the combined work force, or 3,000 jobs, will be eliminated.

- Cost reductions and branch consolidations
  will be realized in both institutions.

Both banks instituted hiring freezes to minimize the number of affected workers. Severance packages and outplacement services will be offered to assist those who are affected by the cutbacks. A charge of $400 million is anticipated to complete the consolidation process.

The biggest challenge for this in-market merger is satisfying regulators that anticompetitive conditions will not exist. To address these issues, Fleet management has indicated that at least $3 billion in assets will be sold. This may include all of Shawmut's $500 million in assets in Rhode Island and some assets in Rhode Island.

Nevertheless, the new entity enjoys top ranking in many categories in the New England region:

- Consumer deposits
- Consumer loans
- Private banking
- Personal trust
- Middle market lending
- Cash management
- Branch and ATM network

The Future

Whether the transaction is an in-market merger or one that crosses several state lines, bank mergers and acquisitions will continue to propel the industry into an ever more efficient organizational pattern. Competitive factors will not subside; they will accelerate. Technology will continue to offer new and better ways of delivering

financial services. Customers will demand a broader
selection of competitive products. Nationwide banking
will complement all these trends. Continued industry
consolidation is inevitable.

Selected References

"BankAmerica Finalizes Terms Covering Merger With Continental Bank," *Wall Street Journal*, August 24, 1994, p. C2.

Covington, Howard E. and Marion A. Ellis. *The Story of NationsBank: Changing the Face of American Banking*, Chapel Hill, North Carolina: The University of North Carolina Press, 1993.

Day, Jacqueline. "Grand Slam (Chemical Banking)," *Bank Systems+ Technology*, April 1994.

Gibson, Paul. "Chemical's New Equation," *Institutional Investor*, February 1994, pp. 54-60.

Glasgall, William. "Troubles of a Model Merger (Chemical Banking)," *Business Week*, November 18, 1991, pp. 114-115.

Hawkins, Chuck, Dean Foust, Zachary Schiller, and Peter Finch. "Super Banker: NCNB's Hugh McColl is Out to Make History with His Bid for C&S/Sovran," *Business Week*, July 15, 1991, pp. 116-120.

Hawkins, Chuck, Suzanne Woolley, and Janet Fix. "Hugh McColl's Masterwork," *Business Week*, April 27, 1992, pp. 94-95.

Holland, Kelley. "Why the Chemistry is Right at Chemical," *Business Week*, June 7, 1993, pp. 90-93.

Jackson, Ted. "NationsBank Buys Big-League Status," *Euromoney*, April 1993, pp. 71-72.

Mitchell, Russell and Richard A. Melcher. "Dick Rosenberg's Manifest Destiny," *Business Week*, February 14, 1994, p. 31.

Rebello, Joseph. "Fleet's Acquisition of Shawmut Caps Chairman's Efforts to Build Up a Bank," *Wall Street Journal*, February 23, 1995, p. B11.

"A Second Act for Walt Shipley," *U.S. Banker*, March 1994, pp. 24-29.

Smith, Geoffrey, Leah Nathans Spiro, Catherine Yang, and Joan Hamilton. "Right Time, Right Place, Right Price (Fleet)," *Business Week*, May 6, 1991, pp.28-29.

Srodes, James. "Hurry Up and Wait: Why Washington Keeps Stalling NCNB's Merger with C&S/Sovran," *Financial World*, November 16, 1991, pp. 27-28.

Wood, Tom. "What Went Right (Chemical Banking)," *Bank Director*, Fourth Quarter 1993.

Endnotes

1 An industrial bank is a state-chartered finance company that makes loans and raises funds by selling investment certificates or investment shares to the public. Industrial banks do not have demand deposit accounts, but many offer NOW (negotiable order of withdrawal) accounts.

2 An Edge Act bank is federally chartered to engage in international banking and is permitted to invest in nonbank financial institutions as along as they are also involved in international operations. The attraction is that these banks are also permitted to operate in states outside the home state.

3 A loan production office takes loan applications and arranges financing for corporations and small businesses, but does not accept deposits.

4 In fact, Florida deposits reached $117 billion by 1990 and $123 billion by 1994.

5 The other two trust companies grandfathered by the Florida law were Royal Trust Company of Canada and Northern Trust Company of Chicago.

6 In 1989, Florida National was sold to First Union, also of North Carolina. At that time, the Florida National management asked NCNB if the bank would like to participate in the bidding. NCNB declined.

7 The price of the Gulfstream acquisition was $92 million.

8 The price of the Exchange Bancorp acquisition was $135 million.

9 These are frequently used alternative names for Federal National Mortgage Association (Fannie Mae), Federal Home Loan Mortgage Corporation (Freddie Mac), and Government National Mortgage Association (Ginnie Mae).

10 Returns on assets and equity for NationsBank have lagged the industry averages for superregional in recent quarters.

11 See the section above entitled "Seasoned Experience and Interstate Expansion."

12 See "Dick Rosenberg's Manifest Destiny" by Russell Mitchell.

13 The holding company assumed the name Banc One, with a "c," because Ohio law restricts the use of the word bank.

Appendix A:
The Time Value
of Money

	Single Amount	Annuity	Perpetuity
When applicable:			
	2 CFs— PV and FV	finite# of equal CFs at equal intervals	infinite # of equal CFs at equal intervals
Future value			
Formula:			
FV =	$PV(1+k)n$	$Pymt[(1/k)(\{1+k\}n-1)]$	n/a
Meaning of n:			
	# of periods after CF	# of payments	n/a

Implied POV:

n periods after CF	same point as last CF	n/a

Present value

Formula:

$$PV = FV(1/(1+k)n)\ Pymt[(1/k)(1-\{1/(1+k)n\})]\qquad Pymt(1/k)$$

Meaning of n:

# of periods before CF	# of payments	n/a

Implied POV:

n periods before CF	one period before first CF	one period before first CF

Legend:

PV	Present value
FV	Future value
CF	Cash flow
POV	Point of valuation
Pymt	Periodic payment
k	Rate of return
n/a	not applicable

Appendix B:
Time Value Tables

B–1
FUTURE VALUE OF $1
$FVIF = (1+k)^n$

PERIODS	1%	2%	3%	4%	5%	6%
1	1.0100	1.0200	1.0300	1.0400	1.0500	1.0600
2	1.0201	1.0404	1.0609	1.0816	1.1025	1.1236
3	1.0303	1.0612	1.0927	1.1249	1.1576	1.1910
4	1.0406	1.0824	1.1255	1.1699	1.2155	1.2625
5	1.0510	1.1041	1.1593	1.2167	1.2763	1.3382
6	1.0615	1.1262	1.1941	1.2653	1.3401	1.4185
7	1.0721	1.1487	1.2299	1.3159	1.4071	1.5036
8	1.0829	1.1717	1.2668	1.3686	1.4775	1.5938
9	1.0937	1.1951	1.3048	1.4233	1.5513	1.6895
10	1.1046	1.2190	1.3439	1.4802	1.6289	1.7908
11	1.1157	1.2434	1.3842	1.5395	1.7103	1.8983
12	1.1268	1.2682	1.4258	1.6010	1.7959	2.0122
13	1.1381	1.2936	1.4685	1.6651	1.8856	2.1329
14	1.1495	1.3195	1.5126	1.7317	1.9799	2.2609
15	1.1610	1.3459	1.5580	1.8009	2.0789	2.3966
16	1.1726	1.3728	1.6047	1.8730	2.1829	2.5404
17	1.1843	1.4002	1.6528	1.9479	2.2920	2.6928
18	1.1961	1.4282	1.7024	2.0258	2.4066	2.8543
19	1.2081	1.4568	1.7535	2.1068	2.5270	3.0256
20	1.2202	1.4859	1.8061	2.1911	2.6533	3.2071
25	1.2824	1.6406	2.0938	2.6658	3.3864	4.2919
30	1.3478	1.8114	2.4273	3.2434	4.3219	5.7435
35	1.4166	1.9999	2.8139	3.9461	5.5160	7.6861
40	1.4889	2.2080	3.2620	4.8010	7.0400	10.2857
45	1.5648	2.4379	3.7816	5.8412	8.9850	13.7646
50	1.6446	2.6916	4.3839	7.1067	11.4674	18.4202

7%	8%	9%	10%	11%	12%	13%
1.0700	1.0800	1.0900	1.1000	1.1100	1.1200	1.1300
1.1449	1.1664	1.1881	1.2100	1.2321	1.2544	1.2769
1.2250	1.2597	1.2950	1.3310	1.3676	1.4049	1.4429
1.3108	1.3605	1.4116	1.4641	1.5181	1.5735	1.6305
1.4026	1.4693	1.5386	1.6105	1.6851	1.7623	1.8424
1.5007	1.5869	1.6771	1.7716	1.8704	1.9738	2.0820
1.6058	1.7138	1.8280	1.9487	2.0762	2.2107	2.3526
1.7182	1.8509	1.9926	2.1436	2.3045	2.4760	2.6584
1.8385	1.9990	2.1719	2.3579	2.5580	2.7731	3.0040
1.9672	2.1589	2.3674	2.5937	2.8394	3.1058	3.3946
2.1049	2.3316	2.5804	2.8531	3.1518	3.4785	3.8359
2.2522	2.5182	2.8127	3.1384	3.4985	3.8960	4.3345
2.4098	2.7196	3.0658	3.4523	3.8833	4.3635	4.8980
2.5785	2.9372	3.3417	3.7975	4.3104	4.8871	5.5348
2.7590	3.1722	3.6425	4.1772	4.7846	5.4736	6.2543
2.9522	3.4259	3.9703	4.5950	5.3109	6.1304	7.0673
3.1588	3.7000	4.3276	5.0545	5.8951	6.8660	7.9861
3.3799	3.9960	4.7171	5.5599	6.5436	7.6900	9.0243
3.6165	4.3157	5.1417	6.1159	7.2633	8.6128	10.1974
3.8697	4.6610	5.6044	6.7275	8.0623	9.6463	11.5231
5.4274	6.8485	8.6231	10.8347	13.5855	17.0001	21.2305
7.6123	10.0627	13.2677	17.4494	22.8923	29.9599	39.1159
10.6766	14.7853	20.4140	28.1024	38.5749	52.7996	72.0685
14.9745	21.7245	31.4094	45.2593	65.0009	93.0510	132.7816
21.0025	31.9204	48.3273	72.8905	109.5302	163.9876	244.6414
29.4570	46.9016	74.3575	117.3909	184.5648	289.0022	450.7359

PER.	14%	15%	16%	17%	18%	19%	20%
1	1.1400	1.1500	1.1600	1.1700	1.1800	1.1900	1.2000
2	1.2996	1.3225	1.3456	1.3689	1.3924	1.4161	1.4400
3	1.4815	1.5209	1.5609	1.6016	1.6430	1.6852	1.7280
4	1.6890	1.7490	1.8106	1.8739	1.9388	2.0053	2.0736
5	1.9254	2.0114	2.1003	2.1924	2.2878	2.3864	2.4883
6	2.1950	2.3131	2.4364	2.5652	2.6996	2.8398	2.9860
7	2.5023	2.6600	2.8262	3.0012	3.1855	3.3793	3.5832
8	2.8526	3.0590	3.2784	3.5115	3.7589	4.0214	4.2998
9	3.2519	3.5179	3.8030	4.1084	4.4355	4.7854	5.1598
10	3.7072	4.0456	4.4114	4.8068	5.2338	5.6947	6.1917
11	4.2262	4.6524	5.1173	5.6240	6.1759	6.7767	7.4301
12	4.8179	5.3503	5.9360	6.5801	7.2876	8.0642	8.9161
13	5.4924	6.1528	6.8858	7.6987	8.5994	9.5964	10.6993
14	6.2613	7.0757	7.9875	9.0075	10.1472	11.4198	12.8392
15	7.1379	8.1371	9.2655	10.5387	11.9737	13.5895	15.4070
16	8.1372	9.3576	10.7480	12.3303	14.1290	16.1715	18.4884
17	9.2765	10.7613	12.4677	14.4265	16.6722	19.2441	22.1861
18	10.5752	12.3755	14.4625	16.8790	19.6733	22.9005	26.6233
19	12.0557	14.2318	16.7765	19.7484	23.2144	27.2516	31.9480
20	13.7435	16.3665	19.4608	23.1056	27.3930	32.4294	38.3376
25	26.4619	32.9190	40.8742	50.6578	62.6686	77.3881	95.3962
30	50.9502	66.2118	85.8499	111.0647	143.3706	184.6753	237.3763
35	98.1002	133.1755	180.3141	243.5035	327.9973	440.7006	590.6682
40	188.8835	267.8635	378.7212	533.8687	750.3783	1.05e+03	1.47e+03
45	363.6791	538.7693	795.4438	1.17e+03	1.72e+03	2.51e+03	3.66e+03
50	700.2330	1.08e+03	1.67e+03	2.57e+03	3.93e+03	5.99e+03	9.10e+03

B–2
FUTURE VALUE OF AN ANNUITY OF $1
FVIFA = $((1+k)^n-1)/k$

PERIODS	1%	2%	3%	4%	5%	6%
1	1.0000	1.0000	1.0000	1.0000	1.0000	1.0000
2	2.0100	2.0200	2.0300	2.0400	2.0500	2.0600
3	3.0301	3.0604	3.0909	3.1216	3.1525	3.1836
4	4.0604	4.1216	4.1836	4.2465	4.3101	4.3746
5	5.1010	5.2040	5.3091	5.4163	5.5256	5.6371
6	6.1520	6.3081	6.4684	6.6330	6.8019	6.9753
7	7.2135	7.4343	7.6625	7.8983	8.1420	8.3938
8	8.2857	8.5830	8.8923	9.2142	9.5491	9.8975
9	9.3685	9.7546	10.1591	10.5828	11.0266	11.4913
10	10.4622	10.9497	11.4639	12.0061	12.5779	13.1808
11	11.5668	12.1687	12.8078	13.4864	14.2068	14.9716
12	12.6825	13.4121	14.1920	15.0258	15.9171	16.8699
13	13.8093	14.6803	15.6178	16.6268	17.7130	18.8821
14	14.9474	15.9739	17.0863	18.2919	19.5986	21.0151
15	16.0969	17.2934	18.5989	20.0236	21.5786	23.2760
16	17.2579	18.6393	20.1569	21.8245	23.6575	25.6725
17	18.4304	20.0121	21.7616	23.6975	25.8404	28.2129
18	19.6147	21.4123	23.4144	25.6454	28.1324	30.9057
19	20.8109	22.8406	25.1169	27.6712	30.5390	33.7600
20	22.0190	24.2974	26.8704	29.7781	33.0660	36.7856
25	28.2432	32.0303	36.4593	41.6459	47.7271	54.8645
30	34.7849	40.5681	47.5754	56.0849	66.4388	79.0582
35	41.6603	49.9945	60.4621	73.6522	90.3203	111.4348
40	48.8864	60.4020	75.4013	95.0255	120.7998	154.7620
45	56.4811	71.8927	92.7199	121.0294	159.7002	212.7435
50	64.4632	84.5794	112.7969	152.6671	209.3480	290.3359

PER.	7%	8%	9%	10%	11%	12%	13%
1	1.0000	1.0000	1.0000	1.0000	1.0000	1.0000	1.0000
2	2.0700	2.0800	2.0900	2.1000	2.1100	2.1200	2.1300
3	3.2149	3.2464	3.2781	3.3100	3.3421	3.3744	3.4069
4	4.4399	4.5061	4.5731	4.6410	4.7097	4.7793	4.8498
5	5.7507	5.8666	5.9847	6.1051	6.2278	6.3528	6.4803
6	7.1533	7.3359	7.5233	7.7156	7.9129	8.1152	8.3227
7	8.6540	8.9228	9.2004	9.4872	9.7833	10.0890	10.4047
8	10.2598	10.6366	11.0285	11.4359	11.8594	12.2997	12.7573
9	11.9780	12.4876	13.0210	13.5795	14.1640	14.7757	15.4157
10	13.8164	14.4866	15.1929	15.9374	16.7220	17.5487	18.4197
11	15.7836	16.6455	17.5603	18.5312	19.5614	20.6546	21.8143
12	17.8885	18.9771	20.1407	21.3843	22.7132	24.1331	25.6502
13	20.1406	21.4953	22.9534	24.5227	26.2116	28.0291	29.9847
14	22.5505	24.2149	26.0192	27.9750	30.0949	32.3926	34.8827
15	25.1290	27.1521	29.3609	31.7725	34.4054	37.2797	40.4175
16	27.8881	30.3243	33.0034	35.9497	39.1899	42.7533	46.6717
17	30.8402	33.7502	36.9737	40.5447	44.5008	48.8837	53.7391
18	33.9990	37.4502	41.3013	45.5992	50.3959	55.7497	61.7251
19	37.3790	41.4463	46.0185	51.1591	56.9395	63.4397	70.7494
20	40.9955	45.7620	51.1601	57.2750	64.2028	72.0524	80.9468
25	63.2490	73.1059	84.7009	98.3471	114.4133	133.3339	155.6196
30	94.4608	113.2832	136.3075	164.4940	199.0209	241.3327	293.1992
35	138.2369	172.3168	215.7108	271.0244	341.5896	431.6635	546.6808
40	199.6351	259.0565	337.8824	442.5926	581.8261	767.0914	1.01e+03
45	285.7493	386.5056	525.8587	718.9048	986.6386	1.36e+03	1.87e+03
50	406.5289	573.7702	815.0836	1.16e+03	1.67e+03	2.40e+03	3.46e+03

14%	15%	16%	17%	18%	19%	20%
1.0000	1.0000	1.0000	1.0000	1.0000	1.0000	1.0000
2.1400	2.1500	2.1600	2.1700	2.1800	2.1900	2.2000
3.4396	3.4725	3.5056	3.5389	3.5724	3.6061	3.6400
4.9211	4.9934	5.0665	5.1405	5.2154	5.2913	5.3680
6.6101	6.7424	6.8771	7.0144	7.1542	7.2966	7.4416
8.5355	8.7537	8.9775	9.2068	9.4420	9.6830	9.9299
10.7305	11.0668	11.4139	11.7720	12.1415	12.5227	12.9159
13.2328	13.7268	14.2401	14.7733	15.3270	15.9020	16.4991
16.0853	16.7858	17.5185	18.2847	19.0859	19.9234	20.7989
19.3373	20.3037	21.3215	22.3931	23.5213	24.7089	25.9587
23.0445	24.3493	25.7329	27.1999	28.7551	30.4035	32.1504
27.2707	29.0017	30.8502	32.8239	34.9311	37.1802	39.5805
32.0887	34.3519	36.7862	39.4040	42.2187	45.2445	48.4966
37.5811	40.5047	43.6720	47.1027	50.8180	54.8409	59.1959
43.8424	47.5804	51.6595	56.1101	60.9653	66.2607	72.0351
50.9804	55.7175	60.9250	66.6488	72.9390	79.8502	87.4421
59.1176	65.0751	71.6730	78.9792	87.0680	96.0218	105.9306
68.3941	75.8364	84.1407	93.4056	103.7403	115.2659	128.1167
78.9692	88.2118	98.6032	110.2846	123.4135	138.1664	154.7400
91.0249	102.4436	115.3797	130.0329	146.6280	165.4180	186.6880
181.8708	212.7930	249.2140	292.1049	342.6035	402.0425	471.9811
356.7868	434.7451	530.3117	647.4391	790.9480	966.7122	1.18e+03
693.5727	881.1702	1.12e+03	1.43e+03	1.82e+03	2.31e+03	2.95e+03
1.34e+03	1.78e+03	2.36e+03	3.13e+03	4.16e+03	5.53e+03	7.34e+03
2.59e+03	3.59e+03	4.97e+03	6.88e+03	9.53e+03	1.32e+04	1.83e+04
4.99e+03	7.22e+03	1.04e+04	1.51e+04	2.18e+04	3.15e+04	4.55e+04

B–3
PRESENT VALUE OF $1
$PVIF = (1/(1+k)^n)$

PERIODS	1%	2%	3%	4%	5%	6%
1	0.9901	0.9804	0.9709	0.9615	0.9524	0.9434
2	0.9803	0.9612	0.9426	0.9246	0.9070	0.8900
3	0.9706	0.9423	0.9151	0.8890	0.8638	0.8396
4	0.9610	0.9238	0.8885	0.8548	0.8227	0.7921
5	0.9515	0.9057	0.8626	0.8219	0.7835	0.7473
6	0.9420	0.8880	0.8375	0.7903	0.7462	0.7050
7	0.9327	0.8706	0.8131	0.7599	0.7107	0.6651
8	0.9235	0.8535	0.7894	0.7307	0.6768	0.6274
9	0.9143	0.8368	0.7664	0.7026	0.6446	0.5919
10	0.9053	0.8203	0.7441	0.6756	0.6139	0.5584
11	0.8963	0.8043	0.7224	0.6496	0.5847	0.5268
12	0.8874	0.7885	0.7014	0.6246	0.5568	0.4970
13	0.8787	0.7730	0.6810	0.6006	0.5303	0.4688
14	0.8700	0.7579	0.6611	0.5775	0.5051	0.4423
15	0.8613	0.7430	0.6419	0.5553	0.4810	0.4173
16	0.8528	0.7284	0.6232	0.5339	0.4581	0.3936
17	0.8444	0.7142	0.6050	0.5134	0.4363	0.3714
18	0.8360	0.7002	0.5874	0.4936	0.4155	0.3503
19	0.8277	0.6864	0.5703	0.4746	0.3957	0.3305
20	0.8195	0.6730	0.5537	0.4564	0.3769	0.3118
25	0.7798	0.6095	0.4776	0.3751	0.2953	0.2330
30	0.7419	0.5521	0.4120	0.3083	0.2314	0.1741
35	0.7059	0.5000	0.3554	0.2534	0.1813	0.1301
40	0.6717	0.4529	0.3066	0.2083	0.1420	0.0972
45	0.6391	0.4102	0.2644	0.1712	0.1113	0.0727
50	1.0000	0.3715	0.2281	0.1407	0.0872	0.0543

7%	8%	9%	10%	11%	12%	13%
0.9346	0.9259	0.9174	0.9091	0.9009	0.8929	0.8850
0.8734	0.8573	0.8417	0.8264	0.8116	0.7972	0.7831
0.8163	0.7938	0.7722	0.7513	0.7312	0.7118	0.6931
0.7629	0.7350	0.7084	0.6830	0.6587	0.6355	0.6133
0.7130	0.6806	0.6499	0.6209	0.5935	0.5674	0.5428
0.6663	0.6302	0.5963	0.5645	0.5346	0.5066	0.4803
0.6227	0.5835	0.5470	0.5132	0.4817	0.4523	0.4251
0.5820	0.5403	0.5019	0.4665	0.4339	0.4039	0.3762
0.5439	0.5002	0.4604	0.4241	0.3909	0.3606	0.3329
0.5083	0.4632	0.4224	0.3855	0.3522	0.3220	0.2946
0.4751	0.4289	0.3875	0.3505	0.3173	0.2875	0.2607
0.4440	0.3971	0.3555	0.3186	0.2858	0.2567	0.2307
0.4150	0.3677	0.3262	0.2897	0.2575	0.2292	0.2042
0.3878	0.3405	0.2992	0.2633	0.2320	0.2046	0.1807
0.3624	0.3152	0.2745	0.2394	0.2090	0.1827	0.1599
0.3387	0.2919	0.2519	0.2176	0.1883	0.1631	0.1415
0.3166	0.2703	0.2311	0.1978	0.1696	0.1456	0.1252
0.2959	0.2502	0.2120	0.1799	0.1528	0.1300	0.1108
0.2765	0.2317	0.1945	0.1635	0.1377	0.1161	0.0981
0.2584	0.2145	0.1784	0.1486	0.1240	0.1037	0.0868
0.1842	0.1460	0.1160	0.0923	0.0736	0.0588	0.0471
0.1314	0.0994	0.0754	0.0573	0.0437	0.0334	0.0256
0.0937	0.0676	0.0490	0.0356	0.0259	0.0189	0.0139
0.0668	0.0460	0.0318	0.0221	0.0154	0.0107	0.0075
0.0476	0.0313	0.0207	0.0137	0.0091	0.0061	0.0041
0.0339	0.0213	0.0134	0.0085	0.0054	0.0035	0.0022

PER.	14%	15%	16%	17%	18%	19%	20%
1	0.8772	0.8696	0.8621	0.8547	0.8475	0.8403	0.8333
2	0.7695	0.7561	0.7432	0.7305	0.7182	0.7062	0.6944
3	0.6750	0.6575	0.6407	0.6244	0.6086	0.5934	0.5787
4	0.5921	0.5718	0.5523	0.5337	0.5158	0.4987	0.4823
5	0.5194	0.4972	0.4761	0.4561	0.4371	0.4190	0.4019
6	0.4556	0.4323	0.4104	0.3898	0.3704	0.3521	0.3349
7	0.3996	0.3759	0.3538	0.3332	0.3139	0.2959	0.2791
8	0.3506	0.3269	0.3050	0.2848	0.2660	0.2487	0.2326
9	0.3075	0.2843	0.2630	0.2434	0.2255	0.2090	0.1938
10	0.2697	0.2472	0.2267	0.2080	0.1911	0.1756	0.1615
11	0.2366	0.2149	0.1954	0.1778	0.1619	0.1476	0.1346
12	0.2076	0.1869	0.1685	0.1520	0.1372	0.1240	0.1122
13	0.1821	0.1625	0.1452	0.1299	0.1163	0.1042	0.0935
14	0.1597	0.1413	0.1252	0.1110	0.0985	0.0876	0.0779
15	0.1401	0.1229	0.1079	0.0949	0.0835	0.0736	0.0649
16	0.1229	0.1069	0.0930	0.0811	0.0708	0.0618	0.0541
17	0.1078	0.0929	0.0802	0.0693	0.0600	0.0520	0.0451
18	0.0946	0.0808	0.0691	0.0592	0.0508	0.0437	0.0376
19	0.0829	0.0703	0.0596	0.0506	0.0431	0.0367	0.0313
20	0.0728	0.0611	0.0514	0.0433	0.0365	0.0308	0.0261
25	0.0378	0.0304	0.0245	0.0197	0.0160	0.0129	0.0105
30	0.0196	0.0151	0.0116	0.0090	0.0070	0.0054	0.0042
35	0.0102	0.0075	0.0055	0.0041	0.0030	0.0023	0.0017
40	0.0053	0.0037	0.0026	0.0019	0.0013	0.0010	0.0007
45	0.0027	0.0019	0.0013	0.0009	0.0006	0.0004	0.0003
50	0.0014	0.0009	0.0006	0.0004	0.0003	0.0002	0.0001

B–4
PRESENT VALUE OF AN ANNUITY OF $1
PVIFA = $(1-1/(1+k)^n)/k$

PERIODS	1%	2%	3%	4%	5%	6%
1	0.9901	0.9804	0.9709	0.9615	0.9524	0.9434
2	1.9704	1.9416	1.9135	1.8861	1.8594	1.8334
3	2.9410	2.8839	2.8286	2.7751	2.7232	2.6730
4	3.9020	3.8077	3.7171	3.6299	3.5460	3.4651
5	4.8534	4.7135	4.5797	4.4518	4.3295	4.2124
6	5.7955	5.6014	5.4172	5.2421	5.0757	4.9173
7	6.7282	6.4720	6.2303	6.0021	5.7864	5.5824
8	7.6517	7.3255	7.0197	6.7327	6.4632	6.2098
9	8.5660	8.1622	7.7861	7.4353	7.1078	6.8017
10	9.4713	8.9826	8.5302	8.1109	7.7217	7.3601
11	10.3676	9.7868	9.2526	8.7605	8.3064	7.8869
12	11.2551	10.5753	9.9540	9.3851	8.8633	8.3838
13	12.1337	11.3484	10.6350	9.9856	9.3936	8.8527
14	13.0037	12.1062	11.2961	10.5631	9.8986	9.2950
15	13.8651	12.8493	11.9379	11.1184	10.3797	9.7122
16	14.7179	13.5777	12.5611	11.6523	10.8378	10.1059
17	15.5623	14.2919	13.1661	12.1657	11.2741	10.4773
18	16.3983	14.9920	13.7535	12.6593	11.6896	10.8276
19	17.2260	15.6785	14.3238	13.1339	12.0853	11.1581
20	18.0456	16.3514	14.8775	13.5903	12.4622	11.4699
25	22.0232	19.5235	17.4131	15.6221	14.0939	12.7834
30	25.8077	22.3965	19.6004	17.2920	15.3725	13.7648
35	29.4086	24.9986	21.4872	18.6646	16.3742	14.4982
40	32.8347	27.3555	23.1148	19.7928	17.1591	15.0463
45	36.0945	29.4902	24.5187	20.7200	17.7741	15.4558
50	39.1961	31.4236	25.7298	21.4822	18.2559	15.7619

PER.	7%	8%	9%	10%	11%	12%	13%
1	0.9346	0.9259	0.9174	0.9091	0.9009	0.8929	0.8850
2	1.8080	1.7833	1.7591	1.7355	1.7125	1.6901	1.6681
3	2.6243	2.5771	2.5313	2.4869	2.4437	2.4018	2.3612
4	3.3872	3.3121	3.2397	3.1699	3.1024	3.0373	2.9745
5	4.1002	3.9927	3.8897	3.7908	3.6959	3.6048	3.5172
6	4.7665	4.6229	4.4859	4.3553	4.2305	4.1114	3.9975
7	5.3893	5.2064	5.0330	4.8684	4.7122	4.5638	4.4226
8	5.9713	5.7466	5.5348	5.3349	5.1461	4.9676	4.7988
9	6.5152	6.2469	5.9952	5.7590	5.5370	5.3282	5.1317
10	7.0236	6.7101	6.4177	6.1446	5.8892	5.6502	5.4262
11	7.4987	7.1390	6.8052	6.4951	6.2065	5.9377	5.6869
12	7.9427	7.5361	7.1607	6.8137	6.4924	6.1944	5.9176
13	8.3577	7.9038	7.4869	7.1034	6.7499	6.4235	6.1218
14	8.7455	8.2442	7.7862	7.3667	6.9819	6.6282	6.3025
15	9.1079	8.5595	8.0607	7.6061	7.1909	6.8109	6.4624
16	9.4466	8.8514	8.3126	7.8237	7.3792	6.9740	6.6039
17	9.7632	9.1216	8.5436	8.0216	7.5488	7.1196	6.7291
18	10.0591	9.3719	8.7556	8.2014	7.7016	7.2497	6.8399
19	10.3356	9.6036	8.9501	8.3649	7.8393	7.3658	6.9380
20	10.5940	9.8181	9.1285	8.5136	7.9633	7.4694	7.0248
25	11.6536	10.6748	9.8226	9.0770	8.4217	7.8431	7.3300
30	12.4090	11.2578	10.2737	9.4269	8.6938	8.0552	7.4957
35	12.9477	11.6546	10.5668	9.6442	8.8552	8.1755	7.5856
40	13.3317	11.9246	10.7574	9.7791	8.9511	8.2438	7.6344
45	13.6055	12.1084	10.8812	9.8628	9.0079	8.2825	7.6609
50	13.8007	12.2335	10.9617	9.9148	9.0417	8.3045	7.6752

14%	15%	16%	17%	18%	19%	20%
0.8772	0.8696	0.8621	0.8547	0.8475	0.8403	0.8333
1.6467	1.6257	1.6052	1.5852	1.5656	1.5465	1.5278
2.3216	2.2832	2.2459	2.2096	2.1743	2.1399	2.1065
2.9137	2.8550	2.7982	2.7432	2.6901	2.6386	2.5887
3.4331	3.3522	3.2743	3.1993	3.1272	3.0576	2.9906
3.8887	3.7845	3.6847	3.5892	3.4976	3.4098	3.3255
4.2883	4.1604	4.0386	3.9224	3.8115	3.7057	3.6046
4.6389	4.4873	4.3436	4.2072	4.0776	3.9544	3.8372
4.9464	4.7716	4.6065	4.4506	4.3030	4.1633	4.0310
5.2161	5.0188	4.8332	4.6586	4.4941	4.3389	4.1925
5.4527	5.2337	5.0286	4.8364	4.6560	4.4865	4.3271
5.6603	5.4206	5.1971	4.9884	4.7932	4.6105	4.4392
5.8424	5.5831	5.3423	5.1183	4.9095	4.7147	4.5327
6.0021	5.7245	5.4675	5.2293	5.0081	4.8023	4.6106
6.1422	5.8474	5.5755	5.3242	5.0916	4.8759	4.6755
6.2651	5.9542	5.6685	5.4053	5.1624	4.9377	4.7296
6.3729	6.0472	5.7487	5.4746	5.2223	4.9897	4.7746
6.4674	6.1280	5.8178	5.5339	5.2732	5.0333	4.8122
6.5504	6.1982	5.8775	5.5845	5.3162	5.0700	4.8435
6.6231	6.2593	5.9288	5.6278	5.3527	5.1009	4.8696
6.8729	6.4641	6.0971	5.7662	5.4669	5.1951	4.9476
7.0027	6.5660	6.1772	5.8294	5.5168	5.2347	4.9789
7.0700	6.6166	6.2153	5.8582	5.5386	5.2512	4.9915
7.1050	6.6418	6.2335	5.8713	5.5482	5.2582	4.9966
7.1232	6.6543	6.2421	5.8773	5.5523	5.2611	4.9986
7.1327	6.6605	6.2463	5.8801	5.5541	5.2623	4.9995

Appendix C:
Mergers & Acquisitions
Software

M&A Software is available to support the decision making process. The central feature of the system involves all aspects of valuation of a potential merger partner or acquisition target. The first component is market valuation of assets and liabilities—that is, the bank's balance sheet equity. The valuation of balance sheet items includes variable-rate loans (with embedded options of interest rate caps and floors), and mortgage-related assets (with embedded prepayment options).

Also included in this valuation is fee income from deposit accounts, non-deposit services, trust activities, bank cards, loan origination activities, asset sales, and underwriting activities. These elements of fee income are valued as assets of the bank being evaluated. In addition, noninterest expense is valued and the result is considered a liability of the bank.

The fourth component of valuation is off-balance sheet positions. In terms of interest rate derivatives, M&A Software prices swaps, forwards, futures, and options. The swaps are valued using the theoretical zero-coupon yield curve. Values for forward and futures contracts are determined by reference to market conditions and attributes of the underlying assets. Option contracts are priced using Black Scholes option pricing model and Black's futures option pricing model. Other off-balance sheet positions that are valued include unused loan commitments, letters of credit, loans transferred with recourse, and when-issued securities.

These four areas of analysis—balance sheet, fee income, noninterest expense, and off-balance sheet positions—provide a comprehensive, objective assessment of the value of the potential merger partner or acquisition target.

M&A Software also facilitates the analysis of profitability in a way that can be easily compared with that of the acquiring bank. This module compares rates earned and paid on all earning assets and interest-bearing liabilities. This analysis evaluates the extent to which leverage is used and the type of leverage, such as core deposits vs. negotiable CDs vs. borrowed funds. Through this analysis, the relative strengths and weaknesses of the two institutions can be evaluated, enabling refinement of the focus of the combined institution.

For in-market mergers, M&A Software also facilitates an examination of redundant branches, one of the most important areas of potential cost savings. To complete the branch-network analysis, M&A Software also includes a module for branch valuation. This feature supports management in determining the optimal branch network for the combined institution. These branch valuations are based on objective variables that measure sales productivity and efficiency.

M&A Software also can be customized to incorporate other features that may be required by the bank.

M&A Software is PC-based and user-friendly. The system is installed on-site by highly trained professionals. On-site training sessions are conducted for all key officers involved in the merger and acquisition activities of the bank. For more information, call Global Bank Research at 502-423-0760.

Index

About the Author

Dr. Hazel L. Johnson is a Professor of Finance at the University of Louisville. She has worked as a C.P.A. and auditor for a Big Six accounting firm, as a bank financial analyst, and as manager of internal audit for a national insurance company. She was formerly on the finance faculty of Georgetown University. Her research has been published widely in the United States and abroad. She has acted as a consultant to more than 35 of the largest U.S. banks and as an advisor to the International Trade Subcommittee of the U.S. House of Representatives Banking Committee.

She has most recently published *Banking Without Borders: Challenges and Opportunities in the Era of North American Free Trade and the Emerging Global Marketplace* (Probus, 1995), *The New Global Banker* (Probus, 1993), *The Banking Keiretsu* (Probus, 1993), *The Bank Valuation Handbook: A Market-Based Approach to Valuing a Bank* (Probus, 1993), *Bank Regulation Today* (Probus, 1994), and *Bank Asset/Liability Management* (Probus, 1994).

9/23